Cognitive Behavioural Therapy

The practical workbook that will help you overcome daily stress and anxiety for physical and mental wellness for a peaceful life and work improvements.

A new version of you in 30 days.

Included bonus: plan with life-enhancing tips

Zane Yardley

Tables of contents

Introduction 6
   1.   Why Cognitive Behavioural Therapy? 6
   2.   Who is This Book For? 7
   3.   How to Use This Workbook 8

Part I: Foundations of CBT 10
   1.1 Understanding CBT 10
   1.2 The Mind-Body Connection 14
   1.3 Identifying Stressors 16
   1.4 Emotional Triggers 18

Part 2: Tackling Stress 20
   2.1 Recognizing Stress Patterns 20
   2.2 Stress Reduction Techniques 25
   2.3 Mindfulness for Stress Relief 30

Part 3: Confronting Anxiety 34
   3.1 The Anatomy of Anxiety 34
   3.2 CBT Techniques for Anxiety 36
   3.3 Challenge and Replace Anxious Thoughts 41

Part 4: Enhancing Physical Well-being 45
   4.1 The Importance of Exercise 45
   4.2 Nutrition and Mental Health 48
   4.3 Sleep: The Forgotten Healer 52

Part 5: Achieving Mental Resilience 56
  5.1 Developing Emotional Intelligence 56
  5.1.1 Understanding Your Emotions 58
  5.1.2 Managing Emotional Reactions 60
  5.2 Boosting Self-Esteem 62
  5.2.1 Identifying Self-Sabotaging Thoughts 64
  5.2.2 Implementing Positive Affirmations 66
  5.3 Setting Healthy Boundaries 68
  5.3.1 Recognizing Unhealthy Relationships 71
  5.3.2 How to Say "No" 74
  5.4 Becoming Adaptable to Change 78
  5.4.1 Embracing Uncertainty 80
  5.4.2 Strategies for Easier Transitions 83

© Copyright 2024 - All rights reserved.

The contents of this book may not be reproduced, duplicated, or transmitted without the direct written permission of the author or publisher.

Under no circumstances will the publisher or author be held liable for any damages, recovery, or financial loss due to the information contained in this book. Neither directly nor indirectly.

Legal Notice:

This book is protected by copyright. This book is for personal use only. You may not modify, distribute, sell, use, quote, or paraphrase any part or content of this book without the permission of the author or publisher.

By reading this document, the reader agrees that under no circumstances will the author be liable for any direct or indirect loss arising from the use of the information contained in this document, including but not limited to - errors, omissions, or inaccuracie

Introduction

1. Why Cognitive Behavioural Therapy?

So, you might be wondering, "Why Cognitive Behavioural Therapy?" Fair question! At first glance, Cognitive Behavioural Therapy—or CBT for those who love a good acronym—might sound like just another psychological mumbo jumbo. but let me assure you: CBT has been around since the 1960s! In short: its existence speaks for itself!

CBT can help to reveal and deconstruct the interwoven connections among your thoughts, emotions and actions. CBT operates on the belief that our thoughts influence feelings which then determine our behavior; so by learning to recognize and challenge automatic, distorted thoughts we can transform both emotional experiences as well as subsequent behaviors.

It provides a practical, hands-on solution to those dealing with stress, anxiety and depression - or simply the rigors of everyday life - by equipping them with actionable strategies they can incorporate into daily life without dwelling in the past. Instead it focuses on what's happening now to make their future brighter.

2. Who is This Book For?

My intention was to design this workbook with everyone in mind - especially since its challenges don't only apply to certain demographics. So whether you are an emerging adult navigating their way through independence for the first time, middle-aged professional dealing with workplace stressors, or senior grappling with life transitions - everyone has something in this book for themselves! This workbook holds something special just for them all.

Let's consider why targeting such a wide audience makes sense: mental and emotional well-being don't discriminate by age, occupation or lifestyle; stress anxiety and other cognitive and emotional obstacles don't take into account your resume or life stage before making an appearance; they are universal human experiences requiring tools, techniques and insights tailored for universal application that are adaptable and actionable - thus the aim of this workbook.

Are you new to psychology or CBT? Don't Worry! This workbook was specially crafted to accommodate novices. It decodes psychological theories into easily accessible language, simplifies complex methodologies into layperson-friendly formats, and applies academic concepts into real world applications - providing a clear roadmap that anyone can follow regardless of background knowledge on mental health topics.

And if you already know psychological principles or self-improvement practices? Even better! This workbook acts both as a refresher and enhancer, diving deeper into well-known areas while opening up previously unsuspected perspectives. Not just an introductory course, this comprehensive guide scales in complexity and depth as you advance through it ensuring you gain new insights, master advanced techniques, and expand your mental and emotional toolbox with new perspectives to enrich it all the more!

As you flip through its pages, think of this book as an organic entity--one that adapts to your individual life circumstances while providing appropriate advice and strategies wherever you may be on your mental wellbeing journey. Think of this book as your dynamic partner in pursuit of living an abundant and resilient life!

Let's move forward now and start our transformative journey? Your journey toward a new and improved you starts right now!

3. How to Use This Workbook

First of all, this workbook is organized into sections, each focusing on an aspect of Cognitive Behavioural Therapy (CBT). For instance, chapters are dedicated to recognizing thought patterns, challenging negative beliefs, improving emotional regulation and applying coping skills. Instead of reading all chapters from beginning to end sequentially, try jumping directly to those most applicable to your current challenges; each one builds off previous ones while offering specific insights and exercises related to that topic.

Within each chapter, you'll find a mix of theory, real-life examples, and hands-on exercises. The theories provide the 'why,' the examples illustrate the 'how,' and the exercises give you a chance to apply what you've learned - that's where magic really happens! I strongly advise taking time for each of the exercises in each chapter (even the seemingly trivial or simplistic ones!). They serve as practice grounds where newfound knowledge turns into actionable skills.

There are actionable tips, or life-improving advice, sprinkled throughout this book that are designed to give immediate and easy ways of improving life. Consider these as quick wins--immediate strategies that offer immediate relief or insights almost instantly. Don't underestimate their power; even small changes can often create huge transformations.

No matter where you stand on your journey to self-improvement, this workbook has something for you. If you're new to Cognitive Behavioral Therapy (CBT), an incremental approach might work well; otherwise feel free to navigate around as desired if familiar. Our goal is to make this journey as flexible and tailored as possible so we can meet you exactly where you are on your path to wellness.

Are you ready to dig in and take control? Your proactive engagement with this workbook is the first big step toward becoming happier and more balanced in yourself. Let's get going!

Part I: Foundations of CBT

1.1 Understanding CBT

Let's jump right in with Cognitive Behavioural Therapy, more commonly referred to as CBT. So what makes CBT unique among all the psychological therapies out there? Well, CBT stands out by taking an action-focused and problem-focused approach; unlike many psychological therapies which only examine your past experiences or offer broad insight into human behavior, CBT instead targets current challenges directly and provides tangible tools to overcome them - true psychology meets pragmatism at its finest!

How Does Cognitive Behavioral Therapy (CBT) Work? In order to understand CBT fully, it's essential that we fully grasp its foundational tenets - chief among which being the cognitive model which suggests the relationship between your thoughts, feelings and behaviors as interlinked entities. Think of these three elements as three vertices in a triangle, where each point influences the others. Your thoughts about an experience can shape how it makes you feel emotionally, which in turn drives actions or reactions from you. An example would be when giving a public speech: If your thought is, "I'm going to screw this up," that can cause anxiety, leading you to stumble over words more frequently, reinforcing that initial fear that you would mess it up - creating an endless cycle.

But CBT is more than that. At its core lies cognitive distortions: these irrational or exaggerated thoughts that distort your perception of reality and make an otherwise inconsequential event seem worse. You might recognize some cognitive distortions like all-or-nothing thinking; catastrophizing; expecting the worst outcome and emotional reasoning as examples. By identifying and eliminating cognitive smudges from your perception of life you'll see everything become clearer!

Let's dig a little deeper here. While Cognitive Behavioural Therapy (CBT) has its roots in cognitive psychology, its "behavioral" component is equally crucial in providing you with effective coping skills for life's challenges more easily - techniques like deep breathing for anxiety relief, progressive muscle relaxation for stress management and activity scheduling for depression are often employed here to quickly extinguish emotional flare-ups and to keep them from returning again and again.

CBT may include exposure therapy for those experiencing phobias or obsessive-compulsive disorder (OCD). Exposure therapy works by confronting, in a controlled environment, situations or thoughts which cause you anxiety - similar to immunizing against it; gradually building resilience over time by experiencing small doses of the stressor can build resilience over time. CBT has gained worldwide praise as it stands up against rigorous scientific scrutiny; one of few forms of psychotherapy widely acknowledged to be successful across a spectrum of mental health conditions.

So far, we've touched upon cognitive and behavioral aspects of CBT; however, it should be remembered that CBT is an ever-evolving field, increasingly incorporating emotional and physiological components as well as mindfulness practices into modern CBT. Mindfulness helps keep us present by keeping track of thoughts and emotions as they happen - offering another layer of complexity to traditional approaches to CBT.

As you progress through these core principles, one thing will become abundantly clear: CBT is both comprehensive and adaptable. Not a rigid approach that fits all, rather it provides you with tools to use as your own personal therapist after closing this book - for life will continue throwing curveballs your way, yet with CBT you'll be prepared to hit them head on.

CBT provides an answer to this question by being structured, goal-oriented therapy with an endpoint in sight. CBT differs from other forms of psychotherapy in that its time-limited nature keeps you on a manageable journey of self-discovery; rather, sessions of CBT are conducted over several sessions during which you work closely with a therapist to identify specific issues, set realistic goals, and work toward reaching them step by step - giving you a roadmap and step-by-step plan to tackle issues piecemeal!

At this point, you may be thinking: "Sounds nice in theory but how does it apply in my daily life?" To use chronic procrastination as an example of CBT application: First identify any thoughts which fuel it - such as being overwhelmed by its magnitude or doubting your capability of successfully completing it - before challenging them with CBT techniques.

Cognitive restructuring can help combat procrastination-related thoughts by dissecting beliefs and gathering the evidence for them, such as by breaking them into smaller, more manageable pieces; or reviewing past achievements where you successfully completed similar tasks - ultimately changing thought patterns away from irrational, evidence-based beliefs to more rational ones.

CBT isn't limited to cognitive change alone; rather, its emphasis is also on behavioral strategies to combat procrastination. The next phase involves devising behavioral solutions against procrastination - whether that means setting specific deadlines, developing reward systems or engaging in time-boxing techniques such as Pomodoro Technique - not simply changing how we think but translating cognitive clarity into actionable steps - not simply knowing better but becoming better!

Understanding these principles conceptually is one thing; applying them effectively when circumstances call is another matter entirely. That's where CBT's homework comes in; rather than typical school assignments, CBT provides tailored exercises designed to put your newfound skills into action in real-life scenarios - whether that be keeping a thought diary for one week noting any instances where cognitive distortions emerge, or actively searching out challenging situations to practice your coping mechanisms. Either way, experiential learning remains at the core of CBT; lasting change seldom results from mere intellectual understanding alone.

As part of CBT, therapeutic alliance is another central concept. While CBT gives you the tools to be your own therapist, the role of an expert CBT therapist cannot be overstated; they serve as your guide through the labyrinthine paths of your mind by identifying cognitive-behavioral patterns you might overlook and offering different perspectives when roadblocks arise. They serve as coaches, sounding boards, sounding boards - sometimes even being there to celebrate all victories no matter how small.

That being said, this workbook aims to simulate that therapeutic alliance as accurately as possible. By engaging in exercises, reflecting on real-life examples and applying strategies discussed, you are effectively taking on both roles simultaneously: that of both client and therapist. By following along with this workbook and doing the legwork yourself - CBT provides both framework and support while you perform its duties - CBT strives to build stronger, healthier and ultimately happier individuals through collaboration between you and mental wellness tools that promote wellbeing.

1.2 The Mind-Body Connection

Ah, the mind-body connection - an area which is both fascinating and essential when it comes to CBT. Your mind isn't just an isolated control center that tells your body what's happening; nope; there's more of a reciprocal relationship here between thoughts, feelings and physiology that works to promote wellbeing or create discomfort.

Let's start off with an example: stress. Imagine that you have an important presentation coming up at work that causes your palms to sweat, heart rate to skyrocket, and stomach to knot up in anticipation. Though stress may lead to physical symptoms like these, research shows it can actually have two-way effects; adopting confident, open posture (often known as 'power poses') has shown to reduce stress hormone levels as well as boost self-confidence levels - altering body stance could change the emotional state in ways that make you feel more powerful thereby decreasing anxiety induced stressors.

That isn't all; let's delve deeper into the idea of emotional regulation through bodily sensations. Have you ever experienced an overwhelming emotion that left you 'frozen'? That is your body's fight-flight-or-freeze response at work; now consider CBT technique called progressive muscle relaxation as a solution: by systematically tensing and relaxing various muscle groups you can effectively "thaw out" that freeze response and make more rational decisions - this process allows your body to help regulate your emotional state allowing more adaptive thinking and behavior - this way your body regulates both your emotional state as well as mental health!

Let's not overlook the impact of exercise on mental health either. While you might have heard the saying, "Exercise releases endorphins," this statement is supported by scientific research. Physical activity is known to stimulate endorphins and other neurotransmitters like serotonin that play an integral part in mood regulation - almost like hitting a reset button for your emotional state! Have you ever found yourself feeling worse after hitting the gym or going for a run only to feel significantly better afterwards? That is exactly the power of mind-body connection!

Mindful meditation combines cognitive and physical elements to promote emotional stability. Focused breathing and mindful observation of your thoughts can change your brain over time - increasing memory retention, self-awareness, and stress regulation areas of the brain. Your mental focus actually elicits physiological responses which contribute to emotional balance.

Understanding this intricate mind-body connection can be transformative when applied to CBT. By understanding that your physical state affects emotional well-being and vice versa, CBT offers numerous strategies that can be employed to address whatever issue may be present - providing more tools with which you can take on life's obstacles head-on.

So next time you find yourself engaging in negative thought cycles, remember that you have the ability to intervene--both cognitively and physically. CBT recognizes this connection between our mind-body experience and human physiology by acknowledging its interdependency.

1.3 Identifying Stressors

First off, let's examine what stressors really are. Stressors don't only refer to external events or situations - they represent your personal interpretations and reactions. Two people might encounter the exact same scenario--say a tight deadline--yet experience different degrees of anxiety due to individual perceptions, past experiences, and coping mechanisms. Therefore, identifying stressors doesn't simply involve recognising external challenges but rather understanding your internal responses as well.

Let's use an example to clarify this point further: work-related stress. Simply calling it "work stress" would obscure all the individual factors that contribute to it; such as micromanagement from your boss, unrealistic performance metrics you are held to, poor team dynamics or long commutes which drain energy before even starting work - each aspect poses its own source of tension, necessitating its own set of coping strategies in order to combat its negative effects.

Recognizing stressors serves a dual purpose. Not only will it highlight specific triggers that elicit your stress response, but it will also give you the vocabulary to express yourself clearly when feeling distressed - something which often happens without us realizing why we feel this way. Pinpointing individual stressors gives us the language needed to express ourselves more honestly both internally and externally - providing a much-needed map for problem-solving!

Now, let's add another level of complexity: chronic vs acute stressors. Acute stressors include single events that trigger stress such as an argument with a friend or misplacing your keys; chronic stressors include ongoing conditions like toxic work environments, financial instability or long-term caregiving responsibilities that persist over time and require sustained and nuanced approaches for management. Acute stressors may often be resolved quickly while chronic stressors require longer term and more nuanced solutions; knowing whether your stressor is acute or chronic can have significant ramifications on how we address our coping strategies - something we will touch upon in future sections.

How can you identify stressors? Keeping a "stress diary" may sound old-fashioned, but it can be extremely useful for tracking stress-inducing instances in your life and documenting what caused them. Over time, patterns will emerge that provide useful insight into not only what stresses you out but also how you tend to react when under strain.

Identification of Stressors This initial exploration lays the groundwork for CBT therapy. Your goal should not just be to list stressors; rather, understand their intricate dynamics - how they impact on thoughts, feelings and behaviors- as a means of exploration that provides the framework for powerful cognitive and behavioral techniques you will learn later.

Are you feeling ready to address those stressors in your life and uncover them? Trust me: the self-awareness you gain here will be essential in mastering CBT techniques we will explore later on. Relax - this journey has only just begun!

1.4 Emotional Triggers

Consider these triggers your emotional hot buttons; little psychological tripwires that can set off a chain reaction of feelings in an instantaneous fashion. Emotional triggers differ from everyday stressors because they're sensitive, unpredictable, and provoke an immediate, intense emotional response in you.

Let's use an everyday example to illustrate this point. Imagine you're sitting in a meeting at work when someone interrupts mid-sentence to make their point; for some this may just be minor annoyance that is easily dismissed; but for someone else this might spark an immediate surge of indignation, perhaps even recalling other instances when they felt ignored or rejected - and trigger memories from earlier in their lives when similar behavior had caused distress or discomfort. That moment marks more than simply interruption; its emotional response also stems from past experiences that created hyper sensitivity to being invalidated - which then manifested itself into strong emotional reactions due to past experiences that created hypersensitivity that makes such interactions even worse.

Consider another scenario. Let's say your friend casually mentions they can't make your planned get-together this weekend; if abandonment or fear of loneliness are triggers for you, even this minor change of plans can quickly spiral into an emotional crisis; you could start questioning their friendship, thinking that nobody really cares for you; that is an emotional trigger at work!

Emotional triggers can be tricky to navigate because they can be so personal. What may seem inconsequential to one person may cause another a burst of emotions due to personal histories, traumas or unresolved emotional issues. A seemingly harmless comment or situation could open a floodgate of memories associated with past experiences; you may not even recognize their existence until after reacting negatively!

How can you identify these emotional time bombs? A self-reflective approach is key. When an unexpected emotional reaction arises, take some time to reflect and ask yourself some questions: What just happened that triggered it; Why am I reacting so strongly; Is this happening again and is this something recurring in your emotional life? In essence, you are playing detective with yourself: unraveling the secrets of your emotional landscape rather than solving crimes!

Let's be clear: the goal here isn't to completely avoid emotional triggers--life is full of situations that can push our buttons--but rather to understand them fully so they lose their grip over you. Once a trigger has been identified, you can then work to reframe its emotional response - an ability we will develop further as we explore CBT techniques and more advanced techniques later. But enough already; let's move along!

As we wrap up this segment, take some time to reflect upon your own emotional triggers. Recognizing them is the first step on a larger journey towards emotional self-mastery; demystifying these emotional reactions so they no longer control you. Stay with us; this discussion is just scratching the surface!

Part 2: Tackling Stress

2.1 Recognizing Stress Patterns

Stress can often be an ongoing theme in our lives; just like that recurring villain from a TV series--just when you think you have defeated it, it pops back up again in another episode! One key element to managing it successfully is understanding its patterns: when, where and how your stress occurs can give a significant edge when trying to manage it effectively.

Let's begin by considering "when." Timing is everything, right? By observing carefully, you may notice that stress often rears its ugly head at certain times or circumstances--for instance

Sunday evening when contemplating work ahead - possibly giving rise to "Sunday Scaries." Or it could occur whenever facing certain tasks such as presentations or meetings - the key here is identifying temporal patterns so you can prepare and strategize for them accordingly.

Consider, for instance, that you have noticed your stress levels increase on Monday mornings - this information can help you plan your Sundays so you can ensure a more seamless transition into the workweek. Perhaps dedicate Sunday afternoons for relaxation exercises, meal prep or small tasks which would otherwise clog your Monday morning. Recognizing when stress arises can open a pathway towards proactive coping strategies.

Let's move on to where. Environment plays a pivotal role in how we experience stress. You might notice certain physical spaces are contributing to an amplified stress response - for instance, is your workplace excessively noisy? Is its organization interfering with your workflow? Environmental stressors might seem minor at first glance; over time though they accumulate into chronic states of stress.

As an illustration of this concept, consider Linda who works in an open-concept office and notices her stress levels rise when trying to focus amid constant chatter and movement around her. Realizing this, Linda decides to experiment by booking quiet meeting rooms for tasks requiring intense concentration and finds her stress levels immediately decreasing and productivity skyrocketing; that is the power of understanding where your stress lies; it allows you to make targeted adjustments that have an immense positive effect on well-being.

Let's now turn our focus towards how stress manifests for you personally; some experience physical symptoms such as headaches or stomach aches; for others, stress may impact their emotions negatively causing them to be irritable or anxious; and let's not forget behavioral manifestations - such as procrastinating tasks altogether due to overwhelming amounts of pressure.

By understanding how stress manifests itself in your life, you can develop an effective intervention plan. For instance, if tension headaches are the source of your discomfort, muscle relaxation techniques could prove particularly effective. On the other hand, emotional regulation techniques might provide better relief.

Recognizing stress patterns involves acting as a "stress sleuth". By gathering data about when, where, and how stress manifests itself, you're trying to outwit it next time it shows up. This is an ongoing process; with each new piece of data that comes in, coping strategies become refined further; as you become better at recognizing patterns, they lose their power over you so you can regain control and navigate life more easily.

We've discussed when, where, and how to recognize stress patterns. By collecting more data on this front, we have come to realize that the more prepared we become in tackling stress head on. But this is only step one in an ongoing journey - next up: crafting customized strategies to not only manage but mitigate its effects - transforming stress from an adversary into something beneficial that might even sometimes prove helpful! More on that in a bit!

So let's move onto "when." Let's say your stress is usually highest around midday, when your team meeting is scheduled to take place at work. Now that you know this pattern is present, consider employing stress-reducing techniques prior to this known stressor; perhaps five minutes of deep breathing or visualizing an optimistic result of the meeting would do wonders in helping reduce tension before entering battle! Being proactive puts yourself in a better position to handle stressful events by giving yourself the tools needed for victory before confronting stressful events head-on - like arming yourself before going headlong into battle!

As an illustration of where to be mindful, let's use Sarah as an example. Sarah is a teacher whose stress levels increase whenever she visits the teacher's lounge - an environment full of negative discourse and venting - which she knows increases stress levels significantly. Recognizing this, Sarah prefers spending her breaks in her classroom where she can decompress and shift her mindset, thus significantly decreasing stress levels. Even slight changes to your environment can bring significant relief!

Now let's delve deeper into how. Recognizing stress' manifestations is only half the battle; becoming hyper-aware of its impacts requires another. Does stress cause snappy responses from you or make concentration difficult? Maybe stress eating has become a problem; once aware of how stress impacts you physically, emotionally, and behaviorally you can devise interventions specifically tailored for yourself.

Take Mike as an example; when stressed he tends to binge-eat. A customized strategy could include keeping healthier snacks nearby when stressors approach or adopting mindfulness techniques to raise awareness around his eating patterns; such interventions become much more effective when tailored specifically towards Mike's individual stress manifestations.

Stress needn't always be negative: sometimes it can serve as an impetus to growth or change. Eustress, which means "positive stress", can be an invaluable ally, propelling you to prepare more thoroughly for job interviews or adding an edge that boosts sports or public speaking performances. Recognizing when stressors actually benefit you adds another layer to understanding your stress patterns - and may even encourage welcoming certain stressors as opportunities for personal development.

As previously discussed, understanding your stress patterns is a complex and ongoing journey. It involves collecting data on yourself, scrutinizing this data to detect patterns, and creating highly tailored strategies to alleviate stress. While eliminating all stress is both impossible and not desirable; rather, the objective should be becoming adept enough at managing it that its hold over you dissipates altogether, providing greater levels of productivity, emotional equilibrium, and overall happiness for yourself and those around you.

Are You Ready to Put This Newfound Wisdom into Practice? As we progress further through this workbook, you'll develop an arsenal of tools and strategies for managing stress and improving life. Know that You are Never Alone on This Journey; Continue Pushing, Observing and most importantly Grow!

2.2 Stress Reduction Techniques

Now it's time to explore some proven stress reduction techniques. Remember these aren't one-size-fits-all solutions; rather they should be seen as tools you can adapt and tailor specifically for your own stress profile. We will cover three primary methods - Mindfulness Meditation, Cognitive Reframing and Physical Exercise are each effective in their own way but when combined together can create an unstoppable trio of stress busters!

Mindfulness Meditation

Meditation has grown from its origins in fringe culture into mainstream medicine for good reason, and mindfulness meditation practices (subset of meditation practices), are quickly gaining ground. Focused around nonjudgmentally observing the present moment without judgment or bias, mindfulness meditation allows individuals to silence their internal dialogue while creating an active state of awareness about being here now.

But, you might be asking, how does mindfulness meditation help with stress relief? A great question! By being mindful, you're effectively taking a step outside the frenzy-inducing thought patterns associated with stress, becoming an observer rather than participant in its narrative. For example, let's say you're nervously anticipating an important work presentation; during mindfulness meditation sessions you could acknowledge all thoughts and emotions without labeling them good or bad; this detachment helps reveal how these transient emotions don't define who you are as people or who you are as people!

Researchers back this up with scientific findings: multiple studies have proven that mindfulness meditation can reduce symptoms of stress, anxiety and even depression. Regular practitioners report lower stress levels, improved focus and an overall sense of well-being.

So how do you begin the practice of meditation? Simply start small: set aside five minutes each day in a quiet space to sit comfortably, close your eyes, take deep breaths, and focus on only your breathing. Your thoughts may wander; that's okay; the key here is not blocking all thoughts but rather recognising when your focus wanders and bringing it back on track with breathing. Over time you may gradually increase duration; guided sessions or apps may prove particularly helpful at keeping focus.

Cognitive Reframing

One powerful strategy rooted in Cognitive Behavioral Therapy, cognitive reframing involves recognizing and then disputing irrational or limiting thoughts to alter negative or distorted thinking patterns that contribute to stress.

Imagine yourself stuck in traffic and late for an important meeting; your first thought may be, "This is terrible; my day is ruined!" Cognitive reframing encourages you to reconsider this viewpoint by exploring whether this situation really is such a disastrous loss - most likely not, and by reframing the situation you can alleviate some of its emotional charges.

Practice includes several steps. First, identify any thoughts causing stress. Next, question their validity by asking yourself questions such as "Is my thought grounded in facts and rational responses to situations?" Finally, replace an unwarranted thought with more balanced or positive ones - without sugar-coating reality but by finding more objective, less emotionally charged ways of perceiving reality.

Utilizing this technique regularly will enable you to become more self-aware about how your thoughts affect your emotional state, which in turn can reduce stress significantly over time.

Physical Exercise

Physical Exercise may seem like an obvious solution, but you might be surprised at what lies beneath. Exercise is one of the best ways to combat stress; not just because it releases endorphins into your system or releases steam; physical activity works on an entirely different chemical level by activating our bodies' fight-or-flight response mechanisms and altering how we perceive situations that cause us anxiety.

Physical exercise, particularly cardiovascular forms such as running or cycling, simulates one of two natural responses to stress: flight. Your brain recognizes you're exerting yourself, and begins regulating stress hormones coursing through your system - as though saying to itself "Ah, we must be dealing with this problem!"

Exercise can provide more than a quick fix; it can actually help balance stress hormone levels for longer. Plus, its benefits go well beyond stress relief - improvements in cardiovascular health, better sleep patterns, increased energy levels and an overall clearer mind are just a few more of its advantages.

So find an activity you enjoy--jogging, swimming, dancing or gardening can all help to reduce stress levels significantly. Aim for at least 30 minutes of moderate exercise on most days throughout the week for best results and you should feel an instant difference in how your stress levels have decreased.

Never underestimate the impact of strong social support networks. Surrounding yourself with trusted individuals can provide vital calming influence during times of extreme anxiety or distress. By having genuine conversations with those we care about, our bodies often release oxytocin - an anti-stress hormone.

But let's be real; venting about your stressors alone won't do. What matters is the quality of the interaction. A trusted friend or family member may offer unique perspectives or practical advice that may ease your situation; sometimes there may not be one, which is okay; simply being heard can significantly decrease stress levels.

Nutrition and Stress

Have you heard of "stress eating"? Of course you have. Did you also know that what we eat can either exacerbate or alleviate our feelings of anxiety and tension? Foods high in sugar and fat may contribute to feelings of lethargy and mood swings - making us more vulnerable to stress. On the other hand, eating plenty of fruits, vegetables, lean proteins, and whole grains is proven to increase energy and enhance mood, providing better management of anxiety.

Omega-3 fatty acids found in fish like salmon have anti-inflammatory properties that may help combat the negative impacts of stress hormones. Magnesium-rich foods like leafy greens may be helpful in improving sleep - another essential element for managing stress effectively.

Creative Outlets

Try engaging in a creative hobby as an off-the-beaten-path way to reduce stress. Painting, writing, knitting or simply doodling are great creative outlets and can put you into what's known as "flow", whereby fully immersing yourself in what you are doing produces feelings of focus, full engagement and even ecstasy that reduce ruminating on whatever stressors might exist in life.

Sarah, an accountant, found solace in pottery making. Although at first she struggled to master it, this activity took her mind off her demanding job and ever-growing to-do list - even during tax season! Over time she noticed her stress levels drop.

Mindfulness Meditation, Cognitive Reframing and Physical Exercise may be your go-to techniques for stress management; but don't be limited by them alone - don't forget about adding Social Support, Nutrition and Creative Outlets as additional ways of relieving tension! Each additional method adds another string to your guitar of life without stress - make your approach unique to you by being flexible, experimenting and making it uniquely your own - because at the end of the day creating a personalized toolkit that works just for you is what matters!

2.3 Mindfulness for Stress Relief

Mindfulness for Stress Relief Now let's dive deeper into mindfulness's application as stress relief, specifically. Mindfulness can be defined as a mental state where one becomes fully immersed in the present moment without judgment or distraction - an effective stress management technique backed by science. So if your looking to bring down those stress levels, sit tight; mindfulness could well transform how you experience daily life.

Mindfulness may be most commonly associated with Eastern philosophy and practices like Buddhism, but its roots go much deeper. Mindfulness as a concept transcends cultures and religions worldwide - various cultures and religions incorporate mindfulness-inspired practices into their tradition, making mindfulness accessible even to people who may not subscribe to any specific faith or philosophy - making mindfulness even more accessible when stress doesn't discriminate between one person's belief system and another's.

To fully grasp how mindfulness can reduce stress, let's dive deeper into neuroscience. Have you heard of the amygdala? It is a small almond-shaped cluster of nuclei deep within the temporal lobe of your brain that acts like an alarm system when something threatens. Your amygdala releases stress hormones like cortisol and adrenaline when something threatens, giving your body the tools it needs for either fighting back or fleeing from any perceived threats that come your way.

Mindfulness offers an effective solution. Studies have demonstrated how mindfulness practices can actually shrink the amygdala - meaning less stress hormones released and thus decreased stress. When practicing mindfulness, your frontal cortex becomes more active when engaged in higher order brain functions such as awareness, concentration and decision making; leading to less reactive stressors and increased capability of managing anxiety when they do arise.

Doing nothing may seem foreign, and sitting still for meditation sessions can be daunting, but that doesn't have to be daunting: start small; even two minutes per day is sufficient if your goal is just practicing being present and mindful for now. The aim is not necessarily achieving complete mindlessness but practicing presence over time - even for short bursts.

Make yourself comfortable by finding a quiet and peaceful spot to sit or lie down, closing your eyes if this feels better, and beginning by taking deep breaths. Focus solely on the sensations associated with breathing--inhalation through nostrils into lungs and exhalation back out again--while exhalation is underway. When your mind wanders off-course (it will!)gently bring it back onto breathing again - no judgment or disappointment necessary, just a simple return to being present in this momentary moment!

Once you feel confident with short sessions of mindfulness meditation, consider expanding your practice with elements such as body scans. Here, mentally scan from head to toe observing any tension or discomfort and becoming more in tune with your physical state as part of mindfulness practice. Keep in mind that the goal here isn't necessarily changing what you see but simply noting it, which often gives valuable insight into stress triggers and manifestations in physical manifestations of stress.

Beyond formal meditation, mindfulness can be practiced throughout your day. From washing dishes and taking walks, to work tasks that seem mundane but require you to be present in the now, practicing mindfulness allows you to fully engage with whatever may come your way and find pleasure in each present moment rather than letting anxiety about the future or regrets about the past creep in. Doing this not only increases efficiency but can turn even mundane activities into rewarding experiences!

As an illustration of this theory in real life, consider Mark, a middle-aged man juggling both high-stress work and family obligations. His stress was having adverse effects both physically and emotionally. After adding 15-minute morning mindfulness meditation into his routine, Mark noticed a dramatic decrease in stress levels, improved sleep quality, and better interactions with family members as he started each day with a more peaceful mindset. This morning ritual gave Mark the perfect way to kick start each day off right.

Emily was a college student coping with exam stress. Through mindfulness practices even just before her study sessions, Emily discovered she could drastically increase focus and retention while simultaneously decreasing stress levels - leading her academic performance to improve and her enjoying learning more than ever before!

Mindfulness for stress relief is more than a passing trend; it's a scientifically proven tool that can completely change how you deal with stress. Dedicate just a few minutes a day to mindfulness meditation or incorporate mindful techniques into everyday activities for stress-busting success.

This exploration has been quite in-depth, yet there's always more to learn and experience when it comes to mindfulness. Just remember, mindfulness is a journey - take your time, be kind to yourself, and embrace its path toward a less stressful, more present life.

Part 3: Confronting Anxiety

3.1 The Anatomy of Anxiety

What Is Anxiety? Anxiety can be defined as the psychological and physiological response to perceived threats or danger, even if those dangers don't currently exist. Anxiety goes beyond simply "worrying; it often enlarges such concerns to an unreasonable degree. Anxiety manifests through many symptoms ranging from mild unease and nervousness to severe panic attacks - from transient responses to specific circumstances to long-term chronic conditions affecting daily life - think of anxiety as like the flashing engine light on your car dashboard: sometimes just hiccups but other times it means immediate repairs are needed!

Have you heard of the fight-or-flight response? This emergency mechanism of your body's emergency systems plays an integral part of anxiety. When your brain detects an impending threat, it sends signals to release hormones including adrenaline and cortisol - two essential stress management substances which were once useful against predators but now may surface when least expected; for instance when going into meetings or giving presentations. While this ancient mechanism was intended for when facing real predators, its application to modern situations often makes you sweat before meeting, or taking place when most unexpected. Your body is getting ready for physical confrontation or swift escape which are typically not necessary in modern stressful situations!

Anxiety isn't solely biological; there's also an emotional component. CBT excels at targeting both aspects of anxiety, including cognitive facets like distortions of thinking or unhelpful beliefs that contribute to anxiety. A constant refrain that you are going to fail, for instance, will likely trigger anxiety symptoms; your thoughts have direct bearing on how your emotional state manifests; this principle forms the cornerstone of CBT; to identify thought patterns rationally we will discuss later.

Have you noticed how your anxiety levels change depending on the people and places around you? Human beings are inherently social creatures, and our anxiety often has a social component. Social anxiety doesn't just involve shyness but can manifest as intense fear of being judged, negatively evaluated or rejected in social or performance situations. Social media further amplifies anxiety by portraying unrealistically flattering depictions which many compare themselves with, leading to feelings of inadequacy or fear of missing out.

As an illustration, consider Sarah, a young professional who recently landed their first managerial role. While on paper she is more than qualified, Sarah can't shake off anxiety over her capabilities and experiences symptoms such as insomnia, nausea and panic attacks due to catastrophizing thoughts like: "What if I mess up and get fired?" or "What if my team doesn't respect me?" Here, anxiety manifests both biologically and psychologically through physical symptoms.

Tim, a high school student with severe social anxiety, shies away from attending social gatherings or group activities owing to his fear. This self-imposed isolation has had serious ramifications on both his social skills and self-esteem - evidence of an anxiety with strong social underpinnings.

Remember, stress and anxiety are distinct processes. Stress tends to be an immediate response to an external trigger and subsides when that situation has been addressed, while anxiety often remains long after its source has gone. That's why it's essential to address it correctly through medications, therapy or lifestyle modifications or all three if possible.

Understanding anxiety's anatomy is the first step to understanding its complex emotional state, with multi-layered roots that integrate biological, psychological, and social factors. Although anxiety may be part of human experience, when left unchecked it can severely diminish quality of life. With knowledge and the right strategies at your disposal you can manage anxiety effectively and lead a life free of constant worry; we will equip you with tools for dealing with it head on in our later sections so as not to inhibit clearer thinking and more focused thought processes.

3.2 CBT Techniques for Anxiety

Now that we understand how anxiety works, let's put together our plan to combat it. Knowledge is power; applying that power is your superpower! To do this effectively, we will explore CBT techniques specifically tailored for anxiety - this provides a toolkit to manage thoughts and emotions more easily. These aren't simply standard CBT approaches that we discussed beforehand--these will address anxiety at its source! Grab yourself a comfy chair and beverage of choice--let's get going!

The Worry Outcome Journal

First up is the Worry Outcome Journal. At first, this may sound counterintuitive: shouldn't I avoid my worries?" However, documenting them can provide crucial insight into how real outcomes compare with initial forecasts. Here's how it works:

- Identify the Worry: Whenever you feel anxious, jot down what's worrying you. Make it as specific as possible.

- Rate the Anxiety: On a scale of 1 to 10, how anxious does this worry make you feel?

- Predict the Outcome: What do you think will happen? Again, be specific.

- Actual Outcome: After the event or situation has passed, document what actually happened.

- Rate the Outcome: Was it as bad as you feared? Better? Worse? Rate it on a scale of 1 to 10.

The Worry Outcome Journal works its magic through side-by-side comparison between your predicted catastrophes and actual outcomes, often showing them to be much less horrifying than imagined by your anxious brain. But more than just a tracking system, it acts as a mirror reflecting disparities between anxious thoughts and reality and encouraging you to challenge and reframe any distortions created by anxiety. Over time, you should see a pattern emerge: fears often do not materialize and when they do come true they often are much less devastating than anticipated.

Thought Challenging

Let's now turn our focus to "Thought Challenging." This technique requires delving deeper into your cognitive processes and questioning the validity of anxious thoughts - kind of like having your own courtroom drama with yourself as both prosecutor and defense.

- Identification of Thought: Be on the lookout for any worrying thoughts as they pop into your head. Analysis of Evidence: How strong or weak is this belief? Explanations Alternatives: Could there be another approach to viewing the situation?

- Analyze the Facts: Now that all the evidence is in front of us, how valid does this thought seem to be?

- Consider Alternative Explanations: Could there be a different way to view this situation?

- Weigh the Facts: With all the evidence on the table, how valid does this thought seem now?

For example, let's say you're anxious about giving a presentation at work. Your initial thought might be, "I'm going to embarrass myself and my colleagues will lose respect for me." Now, challenge this thought. Have you successfully given presentations before? Do you have expertise in the subject matter? Are your colleagues genuinely the type to lose respect over a single presentation? As you weigh the evidence, you may find your initial thought lacks substantive proof, enabling you to shift towards a more balanced, rational viewpoint

The Decatastrophizing Technique

Let's move on to "Decatastrophizing," or as I like to refer to it, "breaking the cycle of doom and gloom." Here, the goal is to put catastrophic predictions through rigorous logic tests in order to challenge them and push back against your catastrophic predictions.

- State the Catastrophe: What's the worst-case scenario that's fueling your anxiety?
- Probability Test: How likely is it that this catastrophe will actually occur?
- Coping Mechanisms: If it does happen, what resources or strategies do you have to cope with it?

For instance, if you're worried about losing your job, first evaluate its likelihood. Are there indicators that it could happen? Should something unfortunate arise that leads to this outcome, think through your options for dealing with it: savings accounts, family and friend support temporary solutions or searching out another job opportunity (even one more suitable than before) may all provide solutions and show that even when disaster strikes it doesn't have to mean the end of everything. By engaging in such exercises you can realize that even when the worst comes to pass it won't necessarily spell doom!

Progressive Muscle Relaxation

Before you panic at the word "muscles," let me assure you: this is not your average gym routine. Progressive Muscle Relaxation, or PMR for short, aims to foster physical awareness as a form of mediation to promote relaxation in our bodies and mind alike. Sometimes our bodies need a reminder to chill out, you know?

- Identify the Muscle Group: Start with your toes or your head and move sequentially.

- Tense and Hold: Tense the muscles in the selected area as you inhale. Hold for 5–7 seconds.

- Release and Exhale: Release the tension as you exhale, feeling the muscles relax.

- Observe: Spend 15–20 seconds relishing the sensation of relaxation.

Theory works on the principle that physical relaxation can induce mental relaxation; like sending an anxious brain a calm message from your body! When feeling anxious, use physical relaxation therapy as an easy and discreet way to restore equilibrium quickly.

Socratic Questioning

Now we will introduce another technique to strengthen your mental muscles: Socratic Questioning. Imagine having an introspective philosophical dialogue with yourself instead of discussing life's meaning or its significance: instead it addresses why anxious thoughts exist in your life.

- Clarify Your Thought: What exactly are you thinking?

- Assumptions: What assumptions are you making? Are they justified?

- Evidence: What factual evidence do you have to support these assumptions?
- Alternative Views: What are other ways to look at the situation?
- Consequences: What are the implications if your thought is true? What if it's not?

For example, if you're anxious about failing an upcoming exam, you might be assuming that failing would make you worthless. Question that assumption—what factual evidence supports this grim view of failure? Could it instead be an opportunity for growth? Probing your thoughts through Socratic Questioning can reveal hidden irrationalities and open your mind to other perspectives.

3.3 Challenge and Replace Anxious Thoughts

Great news if you're still here! By now, you have your arsenal of techniques for dealing with anxiety in place, each offering something special to the mix. But did you know there is also an effective technique called Challenge and Replace that can attack anxiety directly at its source - like those annoying, troubling thoughts that surface like ads popping up on your browser. While its name might sound simple enough, don't be fooled; its power lies within its simplicity!

Cognitive psychology forms the cornerstone of this idea, wherein we believe it is our interpretations of situations that cause anxiety. If someone you had been conversing with suddenly excuses themselves without warning, your initial reaction may be, "They must think I must be boring", creating anxiety within yourself despite possibly having had an urgent call or something important come up that prevented further interaction between you two. Your thought process rather than the situation itself are ultimately responsible for any sense of rejection and anxiety you feel at social events.

Step One: Spotting the Intruder

To start, become your own mental detective. Without awareness, it is impossible to challenge thoughts that reside at the back of our consciousness and cause discomfort. Journaling can be helpful; every time anxiety strikes, write down what thought caused it - almost like taking a picture of the criminal at their crime scene!

Step 2: Interrogation Time

Now that you've identified the thought, it's time for a mental courtroom drama. Cross-examine this thought like a pro lawyer. Is it based on facts? Is it a rational thought? Or is it an irrational fear magnified by your mind? Ask yourself:

- What's the evidence that supports this thought?
- Are there any alternative explanations?
- What would you tell a friend who had this thought?

For instance, if your anxious thought is "I'll mess up the presentation," ask yourself how this feeling has its foundation; past performances or feelings alone? Sometimes these anxious thoughts don't amount to anything more substantial than a soap bubble! They quickly dissipate with no trace.

Step 3: Replacing the Offenders

Once you have identified and understood your anxious thought, it's time to replace it with more reasonable and rational thoughts. Imagine this like swapping out an engine part: take out what doesn't work and install something more functional; for example if your original thought was "I am going to lose my job because of my late assignment submission", consider replacing this fearful thought with this more realistic and rational one: talk with your supervisor, explain your situation, work out solutions together - one hiccup doesn't define my entire career!"

Step 4: Evidence Gathering

Once you've replaced an anxious thought with rational ones, it is essential to gather evidence supporting them. This doesn't just involve convincing yourself in the moment; rather it involves creating an evidence-backed database of rational thoughts which you can refer back to when an anxious thought resurfaces in your mind - you will then have counter arguments ready.

If, for instance, you have changed your mindset from "I'm going to be alone forever" to "I have meaningful relationships and opportunities to meet people", actively look for evidence supporting that rational belief. Engage with friends, initiate plans or attend social events - even if just on Zoom catch-up! Every positive interaction provides evidence supporting this perspective.

Step 5: Regular Revisions

Consistency is key here - this process should not be an isolated one-and-done experience. Revisit your journal or mental notes regularly to incorporate any new experiences or insights gleaned. Consider it like preventative maintenance for your mental machinery: the more frequently you challenge and replace anxious thoughts, the easier it will become until eventually becoming an enjoyable mental habit.

Imagine Sarah is terrified of public speaking. Before any presentation, her first thought is often, "I'm going to embarrass myself". To combat her anxiety, Sarah writes down this thought and questions its veracity - for instance asking herself whether a minor stutter counts as embarrassment! Instead she replaces it with, "I'm prepared and I can handle this" which then becomes part of her mindset when taking the stage - eventually becoming part of her routine and eventually losing its grip over time.

And that concludes the "Challenge and Replace" technique. From identifying anxious thoughts to replacing them with rational alternatives and gathering real-world evidence, each step in this mental chess game aimed at dismantling anxiety-inducing ones has been designed to decrease anxiety levels. While we will cover even more ways to bolster mental resilience soon enough, take some time now to recognize yourself for doing an outstanding job; the best is yet to come!

Part 4: Enhancing Physical Well-being

4.1 The Importance of Exercise

We have discussed much about mental wellbeing, but let's not overlook its connection with physical wellness. You've no doubt heard the saying: "A healthy mind in a healthy body" right? Well it is not simply an empty phrase - this statement has its basis in science and years of research. So why does exercise play such an integral part not just physical but also mental wellbeing? Stay tuned - let's dive deeper!

Exercise releases endorphins, your body's natural mood-lifters. Additionally, exercise helps regulate cortisol - the stress hormone. However, more importantly exercise has shown to improve various brain functions like memory, attention, and problem-solving capabilities - so for anyone saying they don't like gyms remember that exercising doesn't have to involve bench pressing bodyweight or running marathons (although these activities could certainly be enjoyable!). Exercise doesn't always need to involve going from gym class to class in order for it all- just try something out - there may be something out there that suits them!

By now, it's clear: Your brain is the center of all thoughts, emotions and behavioral patterns. But did you know that regular exercise can also alter its neural pathways positively? Physical activity leads to changes in both structure and function that make your brain more resilient against stress, making your mental muscles tougher to withstand life's challenges more effectively. Exercise makes your brain tougher: better equipped for dealing with challenges in daily life!

"But which exercise should I choose?" You might be asking. Different exercises have different impacts, not only physically but also on your mental wellbeing.

- Aerobic Exercise: Think running, cycling, or swimming. These types of exercises have been linked to reduced anxiety and depression. They help improve not just your cardiovascular health but also your mood.

- Strength Training: Don't under-estimate the benefits of lifting some weights! Strength training can give you an empowering sense of power - both physically and psychologically.

- Yoga: This ancient practice goes far beyond intricate poses; yoga combines physical movement with mindfulness meditation, helping you become aware of both your body and thoughts simultaneously - providing two benefits for mental wellness at once!

- High-Intensity Interval Training (HIIT): If you want an efficient yet fast workout, HIIT may be just what's needed to get it over quickly and effectively. Studies have revealed that it releases higher levels of endorphins compared to other forms of exercise - but consult a healthcare provider first if you're new at exercise!

Before signing up for a gym membership or purchasing running shoes, keep this in mind: consistency is key. A single day of exercise might provide temporary satisfaction; but its real advantages only appear over time. Set achievable goals and make exercise part of your lifestyle; even 20-30 minutes of moderate activity each day can make a difference!

As you add exercise into your everyday life, make a point to monitor how it affects your mental state. Are you finding it easier to focus? Acknowledging any successes along the way can serve as motivation to keep living a healthier lifestyle.

CBT employs cognitive distraction techniques like exercise to manage stress and anxiety. For example, "runner's high" describes an effect of being completely immersed in an activity that allows less room for stressful thoughts to enter your mind; you become present, focused, and happier as a result.

Exercise is one great way of building self-efficacy. Once you begin seeing physical improvements like increased stamina, toned muscles or even weight loss--your sense of empowerment grows quickly and continues into other aspects of life, further reinforcing CBT cognitive restructuring efforts.

CBT requires active engagement and dedication from its practitioners; similarly, exercise does too. By adhering to an exercise routine regularly, it demonstrates your ability to make a commitment and see it through. This trait transfers well to mental health goals; being accountable for physical well-being also builds greater accountability towards mental wellbeing goals.

No one's asking you to become the next Olympic athlete here; rather, the objective is for exercise to become part of your lifestyle rather than something you need to check off a list. Exercise should become part of the journey just like CBT practices are: start small - perhaps with daily 10-minute walks--and slowly increase intensity over time until it seamlessly integrates with your life and can become part of everyday routine. Remember to celebrate all those small victories; they add up!

Exercise, particularly endurance-based activities like long distance running, swimming or cycling builds mental toughness - pushing through physical discomfort while breathing deeply to focus on reaching your goal is all part of CBT-induced emotional resilience building.

Sarah had struggled with social anxiety for some time now, making work meetings an unpleasant experience. A friend suggested trying kickboxing classes; at first hesitant, Sarah agreed and found herself immersed in its intense, fast-paced environment that demanded her full concentration - thus helping both her become fitter as well as reduce her levels of stress and anxiety. Over time both goals were accomplished simultaneously!

Tom was experiencing midlife existential dread, questioning both his career and personal accomplishments. Yoga provided relief by connecting his body and mind more effectively - giving him peace and clarity as his practice deepened.

4.2 Nutrition and Mental Health

Ever heard the expression, "you are what you eat?" Well, it turns out it goes much deeper than just physical appearance; what we consume has an enormous influence on our minds and subsequently mental wellbeing. Let's dive deep together and understand this complex relationship more thoroughly:

this is where Cognitive Behavioral Therapy (CBT) meets dinner plates!

Let's begin with something geeky--neurotransmitters. Most of us are familiar with these chemical messengers that regulate our mood, emotions, and even sleep; serotonin and dopamine being just two examples. Not just your brain makes these neurotransmitters; your gut does too - hence their nickname of the second brain! Foods high in amino acids, vitamins, and minerals serve as raw material for neurotransmitter production - lacking essential nutrients may send your mood reeling inexorably downward like a roller coaster ride!

Blood sugar levels can be like an emotional rollercoaster: Highs and lows can lead to mood swings, irritability and fatigue; foods high in sugar or simple carbs like doughnuts may give a quick energy boost but then cause you to crash both physically and emotionally afterwards. Therefore, eating small balanced meals throughout the day is key in maintaining stable mood levels - both emotionally and physiologically!

Chronic inflammation can be a true eye-opener. Imagine radio static, only with your own brain instead. Trans fats, sugar, and artificial additives all play their part; while anti-inflammatory foods such as leafy greens, berries, and fatty fish act like natural defoggers.

Remember Emily? We discussed her earlier when discussing stressors. Emily experienced dramatic mood swings throughout the day and initially believed it to be due to stress alone. A closer examination revealed she skipped breakfast, had fast food for lunch, and indulged in sugary snacks - once Emily revised her meal plan by including more balanced and nutrient-rich foods she noticed an immediate difference both in terms of mood as well as mental clarity.

This subject could fill an entire book, so let's try to condense it. Have you ever experienced what is known as having "gut feeling?" There's a reason this expression exists; food plays a pivotal role in communication between gut and brain. Probiotics and prebiotics don't just aid digestion - they also promote mental well-being by improving gut flora, which makes you emotionally resilient.

Are you having trouble with focus or memory problems? Nutrition may be the solution; foods rich in antioxidants, healthy fats, vitamins, and minerals provide energy and provide protection against brain diseases while helping improve brain function and cognitive behavior - potentially making CBT practices much more successful!

There's another layer to the "you are what you eat" conundrum: emotional eating. When feeling down, reaching for comforting tubs of ice cream or bags of chips can provide temporary solace - but in the long run can have detrimental consequences both physically and mentally. CBT can provide invaluable assistance by helping identify emotional triggers and replacing them with healthier ways of managing emotions.

Should You Drink More Water for Mental Wellness? Of course! Dehydration can wreak havoc with cognitive functions and emotional regulation, leading to mood swings and fatigue. A glass of water might not be a panacea, but it comes pretty close.

Show of hands? What you may not realize is that what you eat can have an impact on how well you sleep; caffeine and alcohol in particular have been known to disrupt sleep quality, which in turn has an adverse impact on mental wellbeing. Foods rich in tryptophan, magnesium, and low glycemic carbohydrates may help improve quality sleep, complementing CBT exercises for greater mental well-being.

Now let's meet Raj, whom we will discuss in more depth in Chapter 8. He relied heavily on coffee as an aid during his high-stress job, unaware that it was exacerbating his anxiety issues. Switching his diet over to herbal tea and water had a calming effect, helping him control his emotional responses more easily - becoming part of his larger CBT treatment plan.

When we seek quick fixes, it can be easy to overlook long-term effects. A pill may temporarily ease anxiety; however, when combined with cognitive behavioral therapy (CBT), a balanced diet offers a more holistic and sustainable solution to mental wellbeing.

Food plays an essential part in social and cultural life; family meals and traditional cuisine all hold emotional meaning that impacts our mental wellbeing. Recognizing these factors while making healthier food choices is critical; its not simply about what's on your plate but how and why that food arrived there in the first place.

Make no mistake; let's act! In one of the upcoming chapters, we will lead you through an engaging exercise to assess and enhance your diet in accordance with CBT goals. Identify food triggers, emotional eating patterns, and more as we uncover all these insights! Stay tuned; it should prove enlightening.

4.3 Sleep: The Forgotten Healer

Sleep should be an oasis of serenity and peace, where worries vanish into thin air while peacefulness embraces you like a soft embrace. But unfortunately, for many of us it can often become far from peaceful; instead it becomes an arena of competition between racing thoughts, tossing and turning, waking up groggy--no wonder our mental wellbeing suffers in return! But have you ever stopped to consider whether the relationship between sleep and mental wellbeing may actually be more intertwined than we realize? Stay with us while we explore this intricate connection further!

Let's be scientific about it for a minute: When you sleep, your brain does some serious housecleaning - like an expert librarian sorting through memories, experiences and new information--from a day's worth of memories, experiences and learning material--and neatly stacking them on shelves. In particular, during Rapid Eye Movement (REM) sleep phase emotional memories are processed, which plays an essential role in emotional regulation; without adequate rest these processes become disrupted leading to mood swings and diminished cognitive functioning - leading to poor mental health as a direct consequence.

Stress hormones such as cortisol are another reason sleep is so crucial. High cortisol levels have been linked to stress, anxiety and depression; adequate restful sleep helps in lowering cortisol levels naturally and serves as a natural stress reliever. Thus if your CBT exercises focus on managing anxiety and managing stress effectively then adequate restful sleep must become part of the plan.

"Eight hours of sleep" may be a common mantra, but quality matters too. A restless 8-hour slumber with frequent wakeups doesn't exactly do wonders to refresh and restore oneself - this is where Cognitive Behavioral Therapy comes into play - certain cognitive behavioral techniques can help you improve sleep quality by changing routines or identifying and challenging any sleep-related anxieties - this chapter covers these techniques in more depth so keep an eye out!

Have you noticed how poor sleep makes you more anxious and irritable? This is not imagined; lack of restful slumber triggers an increase in amygdala activity (the emotional center of the brain), making you more susceptible to stress and anxiety. Unfortunately, it creates an inexorable cycle: your elevated anxiety makes sleeping difficult; thus compounding itself by poor rest. Breaking this vicious circle is crucial; proper sleep hygiene combined with CBT may prove instrumental in doing just that.

Let's consider Emily, a young professional juggling high-stress work and social commitments, while experiencing restless nights filled with constant wakeups and nightmares. Naturally, Emily's mental health began to decline as a result. Soon enough she realized that poor sleep was amplifying anxiety and depressive symptoms - thanks to both sleep-focused cognitive behavioral therapy exercises and medication she began seeing improvements not only in her sleeping patterns but also overall emotional well-being.

Your bedroom should be a relaxing sanctuary that encourages your brain to rest and recharge. An optimal sleeping environment consists of a comfy mattress, blackout curtains and maybe some relaxing music to set the right ambiance for sleep. A well-curated sleep environment has been shown to have profound impacts on mental health; in fact, CBT approaches are dedicated to optimizing one's sleeping environment (we'll get into all the details in another chapter).

Your internal body clock, also known as your circadian rhythm, controls when and how much sleep is necessary to feel awake or sleepy. Any disruption of this rhythm--be it irregular sleep schedules or night shifts--can wreak havoc with our mental wellbeing. How do we align sleep patterns with natural circadian rhythms? Lifestyle adjustments combined with cognitive behavioral therapy (CBT) techniques tailored specifically to regulate your internal clock. We will cover more about this topic later!

Sleep issues don't just revolve around insomnia; in fact, there's a wide array of disorders that can negatively impact our mental wellbeing. Sleep apnea, restless leg syndrome and narcolepsy all reduce sleep quality as well as contributing to stress, anxiety and depressive symptoms - proper diagnosis and personalized treatment plans for each are key for optimum health; some disorders can even be managed or relieved with cognitive behavioral therapy interventions like those we'll explore later on this page.

Sleep is more than just an evening ritual--it plays an integral role in mental well-being and CBT success. By addressing sleep issues and using tailored CBT strategies to break cycles of poor rest and poor mental health, preventing poor sleeping from compounding further and creating negative cycles. Sleep should set the scene for mental healing each night!

Part 5: Achieving Mental Resilience

5.1 Developing Emotional Intelligence

Ah, emotional intelligence! The secret sauce to making life simpler and more fulfilling. But what is emotional intelligence exactly? Emotional intelligence refers to your ability to recognize, understand, manage, and use your own emotions as well as those around you in an effective manner - not simply being "in touch" with feelings; emotional intelligence allows us to leverage that awareness towards fostering better relationships, reaching personal goals more quickly, and increasing overall well-being.

Emotional intelligence serves as your emotional GPS, providing guidance through social interactions and personal decisions. Why is emotional intelligence so crucial? Because emotions have the ability to get the better of us at times, leading us down paths we later regret taking - emotional intelligence provides protection against such missteps.

"Why bother worrying about emotional intelligence now?" It may be tempting to assume this, but consider this: developing emotional intelligence could transform average relationships into extraordinary ones; average performance into outstanding work; daily stress into manageable pressure - not to mention impulsively reacting or responding thoughtfully when faced with challenging situations.

So where should we begin? Emotional intelligence can be broken down into five key components: self-awareness, self-regulation, motivation, empathy and social skills. Each of these plays an integral part in emotional intelligence but for now let's focus on its broader aspects.

Emotional intelligence may seem like a modern term, but its roots date back centuries. Researchers like Peter Salovey and John D. Mayer were among the pioneers who pioneered this subject. Daniel Goleman later popularized it through his 1995 book entitled 'Emotional Intelligence."

Goleman made a point of emphasizing the fact that IQ alone doesn't determine human intelligence. While your ability to crunch numbers or comprehend complex theories might equip you for some tasks, such as handling heated arguments or managing workplace dynamics effectively, emotional intelligence provides another form of insight and can enrich both your life and interactions with others.

Neuroscientifically speaking, emotional intelligence is more than an abstract concept - it has tangible roots in our brains. Your amygdala plays an integral part in processing emotions while the prefrontal cortex regulates them; when these two brain regions collaborate effectively you're more likely to excel at emotional intelligence.

Take, for example, when someone cuts you off in traffic: the amygdala could trigger a "fight or flight" response--in this instance anger. But with an active prefrontal cortex in place, you could interpret this event differently; perhaps considering that the other driver could be rushing to an emergency or simply made a mistake can help change how we react emotionally - possibly even preventing road rage altogether!

So how does all this translate to real-world benefits? Consider your last experience leading a team project at work or organizing a family event; orchestrating multiple people each with their unique viewpoints and emotional responses can be like orchestrating a symphony. Tuning into your emotional state can help regulate responses to stressors more effectively, leading to better leadership performance; similarly recognizing when team members become stressed or disengaged allows timely intervention for improved group dynamics.

Don't take my word for it; research supports the benefits of emotional intelligence. Studies have proven a direct relationship between high emotional intelligence levels and improved mental health, increased job performance and leadership capabilities - not simply "feeling good", but truly maximizing potential in all areas of life.

5.1.1 Understanding Your Emotions

Once you realize the value of emotional intelligence, step one is understanding yourself emotionally. But before you dismiss this step as too emotional or "touchy-feely", remember it doesn't need to be some soft touchy-feely thing: without understanding what feelings arise for us as individuals, how can we effectively manage or use them effectively?

Let's break down what emotions are in greater detail. Imagine this: Walking down an alley at night when footsteps approach, your heart races and palms sweat; fear arises. Your sensory organs send data to your brain which processes it to trigger an emotional response such as fear. Plus, adrenaline releases from your system as your mind prepares itself to react swiftly - creating an overall reaction of mental and physical panic that has many sides: mental as well as physical!

Do you recognize all your emotions, or can they easily identify what they're feeling at any given moment? Generally, people can identify basic emotions like happiness, sadness, anger or fear fairly easily - yet more complex feelings such as feeling jealous vs envious or confident/arrogant can be difficult to identify accurately.

The next time you feel an overwhelming wave of emotion, take a few seconds to identify it accurately. Is it frustration, disappointment, anger? Identifying emotions accurately will enable you to better handle and communicate them more easily with others - two key components of healthy relationships.

Do you know the term 'emotional granularity'? It refers to your ability to differentiate among closely related emotions. While this doesn't necessitate sounding like an emotional thesaurus with complex terms like 'morose' and 'ebullient,' by expanding your vocabulary beyond simply "good" and "bad," you will gain greater insight into yourself and your emotional landscape.

There's a subtle distinction between feeling "happy" and feeling "content." The former could come from an event such as passing an exam, while contentment refers to more general feelings of well-being. By becoming more mindful of these differences, you are more likely to take steps that foster those positive emotions rather than leaving their development solely up to chance.

Imagine you are in a relationship, and have just had an argument with your partner. Before reacting impulsively, try pinpointing what emotion is really at play: angry at what they think they did or hurt over being dismissed? Once identified, accurately expressing these emotions leads to more constructive discussions rather than heated arguments.

Understanding your emotions requires more than a one-off exercise - it's an ongoing journey that demands your full focus and introspection. By investing time in this effort, you are creating the basis of emotional intelligence - an investment worth making!

5.1.2 Managing Emotional Reactions

Let's keep this momentum going! Hopefully you have become adept at identifying your emotions; that is a wonderful accomplishment in itself! However, understanding what emotions you're feeling is only half the battle; now comes managing them effectively! Recognizing anxiety may be one thing; managing it effectively is another altogether different matter entirely! So, how should we go about doing this?

Self-regulation may sound complicated, but it's actually an intuitive concept: your ability to control disruptive emotions and redirect impulsive behavior is at the heart of self-regulation. For example, when driving late for an important meeting and someone cuts you off in traffic, your initial impulse may be to unleash an outburst of honks or more aggressive language; however, self-regulation serves as the inner voice that reminds you to take a deep breath and stay calm, reminding you that road rage won't help get to your destination any faster.

Mindfulness has its place in emotional intelligence as well. By practicing it regularly, mindfulness allows you to become more self-aware of your thoughts and emotions as they occur, giving you the chance to choose how you'll react when something like your partner forgetting the trash occurs; rather than acting immediately when this happens again, practicing mindful awareness gives you time to pause, reflect upon what's bothering you, and come up with more measured, often more effective actions to take.

Have you ever considered "flipping the narrative?" This involves replacing negative thoughts with more balanced or positive ones consciously. Say, for instance, your boss assigns you an ambitious project; rather than thinking to yourself "I can never finish this on time; it's impossible," try replacing this thought process with "This will be tough but also an opportunity for growth and proof". The emotional cascading effect can be incredible.

Take this example: When engaged in an angry argument with a friend who accuses you of always being selfish, your instinct may be to defend yourself defensively. But use your newly developed emotional awareness to assess what emotion you're feeling: anger? humiliation? Once identified, use a calming technique such as taking three deep breaths or counting out loud 10 times before responding rationally and thoughtfully to any future situations that arise.

Don't underestimate the power of simple behavioral adjustments. Learning relaxation techniques such as deep breathing or progressive muscle relaxation can do wonders to ease anxiety. Imagine you're giving a public speech; nervous palms sweaty: employing these techniques could counteract your body's stress response and make delivering an unforgettable presentation easier than ever before!

Maintaining emotional control requires ongoing dedication and hard work, much like tending a garden. Once you've identified your emotions, the task becomes one of nurturing, tending and occasional pruning out weeds from this new garden of emotional wellbeing. Over time you'll notice both an improved inner landscape and fulfilling external life.

5.2 Boosting Self-Esteem

Hey amazing reader! Let's have an open conversation about something we all yearn for but sometimes take for granted: an enhanced sense of self-esteem. Emotional intelligence doesn't just focus on understanding and managing feelings - it also affects how you view yourself! So let's get talking!

Let's first define self-esteem: some may mistake it for simply feeling good about oneself, but self-esteem goes much deeper. Self-esteem involves appreciating your worth as an individual while taking pride in your skills and accomplishments; it forms the basis of a fulfilling life. Yet excessive positivity may actually backfire by blocking areas for growth that exist - instead, balanced self-esteem should be our goal.

Ever notice how we tend to be our own harshest critics? After all, no one would talk back like that to their friends if we did the same! One way to improve self-esteem and boost self-compassion is through kindness towards oneself - treat yourself with the same respect you would give a close friend when making mistakes - when engaging in self-criticism take a moment and think "If this were someone I cared about making this error instead" rather than indulging in trash talk against yourself! Instead, imagine it was one of your closest friends making this mistake - who would respond by saying something like: "Well it must have been because you simply are the worst!"?

Imagine: Sticky notes covering your mirror, each bearing an affirmation such as, "I am confident" or "I deserve love and joy." Sounds corny? Sure; however, affirmations serve as mini pep talks to reinforce positive beliefs about yourself. Make it part of your morning ritual to read out a few affirmations each morning, and you'll soon discover just how effective these short phrases can be at setting an upbeat, optimistic tone for the day ahead.

Compare and Contrast... that dreaded game. Admit it, how often have you found yourself scrolling social media feeling increasingly down on yourself? Measuring yourself against someone else's highlight reel can only set yourself up for failure; remember, each individual journey and setback brings unique challenges and accomplishments that simply cannot be compared against one another.

Imagine believing you were hopelessly terrible at math and there was nothing you could do about it; that's the fixed mindset in action. Now think about believing that with some effort and persistence you could improve - that's the growth mindset! Just this simple change alone will do wonders for your self-esteem as challenges will now be seen as opportunities rather than hurdles to be overcome.

Take a step back from social media, focus on yourself, and enjoy some solitude. A social media detox isn't just trendy; it can also be soul-refreshing. Reducing online consumption helps break out of comparison's cycle while opening up avenues towards genuine self-improvement.

Celebrating small achievements gives us tangible ways to see just how awesome we really are; don't wait for some monumental accomplishment to reward yourself; take small victories as milestones on your path toward growth! Recognizing and appreciating small victories gives you a tangible way to realize how awesome you truly are; do so now.

Implementing these principles into your life won't just boost your self-esteem; they'll have ripple effects throughout every area of your life - from relationships to careers.

5.2.1 Identifying Self-Sabotaging Thoughts

Now let's tackle something we all do but rarely admit: self-sabotage. Your mind might sometimes play tricks on you and lead down a rabbit hole of negativity and doubt; to overcome this obstacle, the first step to overcome this self-destructive thought cycle is recognizing destructive thoughts - trust me; it will feel liberating! So let's dive right in.

Self-sabotaging thoughts are defined as thoughts which obstruct our ability to achieve our goals and aspirations, from directly negative statements like, "I can't do this," to more subtle forms of doubt such as, "I am not good enough." But sometimes these self-defeating thoughts become so deeply embedded that you don't even realize you have them - like they become part of the scenery in your mental landscape!

Have you ever felt like an impostor at work or social gatherings despite performing well? You could be suffering from impostor syndrome. This manifests itself through fear of exposure as "fraud", leading to hesitation, procrastination or avoiding opportunities altogether. Now is the time to recognize it for what it truly is: an imaginary fear your mind is projecting onto you.

Ah, the timeless pitfall. Ever thought to yourself: "If I can't do it perfectly, then it's not worth doing at all"? This all-or-nothing thinking sets you up for failure as life rarely offers black or white solutions.

Imagine this: when something minor goes wrong, and all hell breaks loose! Catastrophizing occurs when we exaggerate issues far beyond their actual importance. Once we recognize ourselves doing this, take a deep breath and remind ourselves that not everything has to be life or death.

Comparing yourself with others is one of the surest ways to damage your self-esteem, with you seeing their successes and wondering, "Why can't I be like them" or, worse still, "I'll never reach their level". These thoughts won't help your goals at all - trust me.

Recognizing when these thoughts occur is key to curbing them early. Perhaps when embarking on something new or being confronted by challenges are they more likely to arise? Knowing these triggers allows you to prepare counterarguments to disarm these negative thought cycles before they take root and cause more anxiety than necessary.

Implement mindfulness into your routine to catch any self-destructive thoughts as they arise. In practicing mindfulness, you'll become an observer rather than participant of your thoughts; thus making it much simpler to identify self-sabotaging ones when not actively engaged with them.

Once you've identified self-defeating thoughts, the next step should be challenging them. Redirect those negative words with something positive; rather than thinking "I can't do this", try saying: "I'll do the best I can and that's fine".

5.2.2 Implementing Positive Affirmations

You might be asking, what exactly is Positive Affirmation? This simple yet powerful statement helps challenge self-sabotaging thoughts by replacing them with more empowering beliefs - but don't take my word for it; science backs this up too!

Positive affirmations are grounded in psychological theory and cognitive behavioral principles, making the use of affirmations part of cognitive restructuring. Repetition will cause your brain to register them as facts over time - similar to deconstructing and rebuilding a home by reconfiguring it with positive thoughts instead.

Not all affirmations statements are created equal; some might resonate more than others with you. If you struggle with body image issues, an affirmation like "I am beautiful just as I am" could ring true; on the other hand, workplace stress requires something along these lines: "I am competent and capable in my abilities". Therefore, to maximize its effectiveness you personally tailor your affirmations statements according to what area(s) they address.

Let's be clear: simply repeating an affirmation won't magically make it come true - you also have to believe it and visualize yourself living it - for instance, if your affirmation involves competence at work, envision yourself exhibiting these characteristics during situations when necessary.

Timing and setting are of equal importance; you don't want to find yourself silently repeating affirmations during a team meeting! A better option would be incorporating affirmations into your morning ritual or during mid-day breaks; this can set a positive tone for the remainder of the day or serve as a kind of reset button.

Try recruiting the help of friends or family as additional accountability partners; make it part of your regular catch-ups, sharing affirmations with each other and discussing how they're helping to transform your thinking patterns. Speaking out loud can make these statements feel even more real and attainable!

There are apps designed to send daily affirmation reminders. Why not leverage technology as a force for good? Set reminders or download an app that meets your specific needs so you'll always have something reminding you to stop, reflect and affirm yourself when life gets busy?

Consistency is key when it comes to any worthwhile endeavor, and repeating an affirmation once may not produce lasting change; rather, its repetition has the power to alter your thought processes over time and change them for good. So keep doing it even when it feels silly or forced - persistence pays off!

Now that you have been practicing affirmations for some time, how do you know it is working? Take time periodically to reflect on your thought patterns: are they less self-sabotaging and do you feel more secure in areas that once felt unconfident? These can all be telltale signs that affirmations is doing its magic.

5.3 Setting Healthy Boundaries

Are My Boundaries Leaky? Ah, the age-old question. If you find yourself feeling constantly depleted and people treat you like an afterthought, that could be a telltale sign that your boundaries may be porous. Other indicators could be saying yes when your inner voice says no and remaining silent when something needs to change; or worse still allowing unwanted physical contact without saying so or speaking up! Recognizing this as soon as it occurs will allow you to take charge of your emotional life!

Not all boundaries are created equal; emotional, physical, time-based and digital boundaries should all be respected equally.

- Emotional Boundaries: Your feelings should always come first - guard them like grandma's secret cookie recipe!

- Physical Boundaries: Personal space is important! Some folks need space while others might prefer an occasional hug - you should know your comfort zone and respect that.

- Time-Based Boundaries: Don't let others dictate when and how you spend your precious hours; be the master of your schedule and stay within its boundaries.

- Digital Boundaries: Boundaries can easily blur in today's age of instant messages and pingbacks; to maintain sharp edges and maintain boundaries effectively you may need to mute, block, unfriend. Our step-by-step guide on crafting boundaries can help.

In order to create your own boundaries you have to go through the following steps:

- Self-Discovery: In order to set boundaries effectively, it's crucial that you understand what motivates and excites you. Write in a journal, or take an honest evaluation.

- Know Thy Limits: Be clear about which elements may cause problems for you in relationships - both potential deal breakers and dealmakers - by setting clear rules about them and understanding when and why certain situations might arise.

- Speak Up: Speaking up can be daunting, but speaking your truth can only benefit both sides. No one's a mind reader!

- Action Is Necessary: If your boundaries have become an embarrassment to someone, take swift and decisive action immediately.

- Check-In and Update: Similarly to software which needs regular upgrades, your boundaries may need adjusting over time as life changes.

If your self-esteem is low, building boundaries may feel like building skyscrapers without scaffolding - but once they're up - even if they look more like picket fences than fortresses - your self-esteem will soar - creating a positive feedback loop!

Workplaces can be a source of great conflict. Not just due to meeting deadlines and taking breaks; there can also be colleagues expecting you to answer emails at midnight and bosses who believe your personal time extends into office hours - this all makes for a delicate balancing act in which one must never lose their sense of themselves or lose touch with what matters to them personally. Juggling should never become an impossible feat!

Romeo or Juliet, even star-crossed lovers need boundaries! It's not unromantic to communicate your needs to your partner; in fact, it can be very healthy! And let's not forget your friends and family - be your own advocate in every relationship you have!

Setting boundaries will inevitably spark some criticism, from side-eyeing or outrage to outright aggression from some individuals, but that should tell you nothing about you; your boundaries are non-negotiable - period.

Let's be clear - relationships and self-esteem are important; but let's not lose sight of one of the main components: mental health. When boundaries are crossed, stress spikes exponentially while anxiety soars! Establishing boundaries isn't only related to relationship management - it's an effective mental health strategy in its own right!

5.3.1 Recognizing Unhealthy Relationships

Now that we understand what healthy boundaries look like, let's focus on something much more challenging but essential: recognizing unhealthy relationships. Here's where emotional intelligence and your newly established boundaries come together to form the basis for effective action plans.

Are You Wondering Why Someone Would Care About My Unhealthy Relationship? Don't take this for granted: unhealthy relationships are much more than mere drama; they're energy drainers, soul suckers and health hazards-- mental as well as physical--that can have lasting negative repercussions in both mind and body. We don't need to get dramatic here: an emotionally toxic relationship can manifest physically through insomnia or stress eating for example.

Let's first dispel a common misunderstanding: unhealthy does not always equate to toxic. People use "toxic" as shorthand for relationships with unhealthy aspects; intent and awareness play key roles when distinguishing toxic individuals from unhealthy relationships; while toxic individuals might intentionally manipulate or harm someone while unhealthy relationships might simply develop over time due to bad habits or poor communication.

Have you ever heard this saying before? Maybe not, but its meaning rings true: anyone with even minimal life experience can recognize an unhealthy relationship if the red flags start flying. Sometimes they're as obvious as an alarm bell in your gut; other times they might simply manifest as vague feelings of unease.

Let's create an emotional health checklist. If too many of these categories apply to you, perhaps it is time for reflection:

- Lack of Trust: Trust is at the foundation of any healthy relationship - without it, the whole relationship collapses into chaos and dysfunction.

- Constant Criticism: Constructive feedback can only go so far; continuous nitpicking should raise red flags. Walking on Eggshells: If expressing your opinions feels like defusing a bomb, we have an issue on our hands.

- Inequality: Relationships should be two-way streets; when one person holds all the power in a relationship, that's no longer partnership but dictatorship.

- Manipulation: Subtle or overt emotional manipulation damages trust and freedom in relationships.

Relationships should be fair. No one should be playing 4D chess moves in the game of love--or friendship for that matter. Be wary of gaslighting, which is a form of emotional manipulation wherein someone causes another person to doubt their perceptions or memories, creating confusion within and doubt in oneself. Gaslighting can be devastatingly effective at discrediting memories or perceptions and leading you to question whether you are going crazy! It is an underhanded, harmful tactic which could leave you questioning whether you exist!

Are All Unhealthy Relationships Salvageable? Nope. But many can be salvaged provided both parties are willing to invest the effort. Sometimes an unhealthy relationship needs a hard reset; like powering down your smartphone when its battery dies out, sometimes your relationship requires you to press 'pause', assess its situation, and then implement necessary changes.

Hey, sometimes the problem lies within ourselves! Sometimes we create unhealthy dynamics. Are you being overly critical, jealous or manipulative? Identifying this as part of the issue is half the battle won.

Let's step back a bit for a second and consider that society often glorifies unhealthy relationships. Have you seen any romantic comedies where the male protagonist pursues his female interest until she gives in? Not exactly the best example to send out as we grow up absorbing narratives that don't exactly promote emotional health - be conscious of any patterns you might unknowingly be subscribing to!

Relationships don't just include romantic ones - friendships can also become emotionally taxing. That friend who always offers backhanded compliments or puts down your achievements may need reassessing.

Family is often one of the hardest relationships to navigate. They may become your closest allies or cause you immense emotional hardships. Establishing boundaries within families may be more complex but is often even more necessary.

If a relationship exhibits emotional or physical abuse, you must immediately terminate it without question or consideration of other options. In cases where it falls somewhere in between, however, one must carefully weigh up their pros and cons of staying. Do you dread spending time with this individual? Or have they made you a lesser version of yourself when being with them? If this applies to you then perhaps distancing might be a wiser option for now.

Not all relationships end on an even note, with an abrupt closure; sometimes it's better to leave things open-ended as both parties grow and change separately. While closure can be therapeutic, allowing both individuals to continue evolving individually can sometimes be therapeutic in its own way.

Once you've identified and severed all unhealthy relationships, allow yourself time and space for recovery and emotional reset. This could range from engaging in an intensive soul search session or professional counseling to simply spending more time alone.

5.3.2 How to Say "No"

Now that we understand unhealthy relationships and their telltale red flags, how do we change their dynamics when stuck in situations we'd rather avoid? Say it out loud with just three powerful letters: NO

"No" is a complete sentence, yet so often we shy away from using it, fearful that its use will offend or make us appear confrontational or awkward. Why is that? Usually it's because society teaches us to avoid conflict as much as possible and avoid confrontation at any cost - at whatever personal cost?

Before embarking on the art of saying no, it's essential to acknowledge the impact of yes. Every time you agree to something you don't want to do, you are saying "no" to yourself; in effect robbing Peter to pay Paul when really your time and energy are being siphoned off by said commitment.

Saying "no" isn't only about saying no; it can also help establish limits and boundaries within work, relationships and even your personal time. Have you ever agreed to attend an event just because it wouldn't disappoint someone? In such situations, saying "no" might have saved the day!

"No" doesn't need to be taken in its traditional sense: It can be flexible, offering alternatives or simply polite but firm responses such as these:

"No" doesn't always have to be a flat-out rejection. It can be flexible, it can offer alternatives, and it can be polite but firm. Here are some variations:

- "I can't commit to this, but I can do ..."
- "Now's not a good time, can we revisit this later?"
- "I'm not the right person for this, but have you considered asking...?"

Let's delve deeper into why it feels so bad to say no, shall we? Our brains are hardwired for social connection as an evolutionary survival trait - being rejected from a group would mean isolation and, ultimately, increased risk of not surviving - when you say no the fear of rejection kicks in and your body releases stress hormones with every utterance - insane!

Remember, saying no doesn't mean isolating yourself from others; it means setting limits. Think of it like this: when you say no to someone asking to enter your emotional and physical space, draw a circle around it to designate its entrance point - your personal VIP area in which only certain individuals may enter.

Have you ever found yourself agreeing to something, only to dread its commitment as it draws closer? Events or tasks which become obligations end up draining your emotional reserves before even occurring; saying yes when one means no is an enormous opportunity cost and should be used more wisely on tasks that align more closely with one's values, needs, or interests.

Of the many difficulties of saying no, emotional manipulation should always be avoided. Others might try to guilt-trip you into saying yes by exploiting fears, insecurities and your desire to appear 'good'; stand your ground and resist attempts at emotional manipulation! Emotional manipulation must never occur!

Let's be real; saying no in work can be challenging, especially to your boss. Yet setting boundaries for mental wellbeing is essential in any professional environment, and respectful communication and offering alternatives may help. If your plate is full, explain your workload and request to prioritize tasks - your boss is sure to appreciate this proactive approach!

At some point in our lives, friends may ask us for favors that we don't really want to do - such as helping move them or attending an event without any interest to you. Don't feel pressured into agreeing - real friends understand and respect boundaries!

Family obligations can be one of the more challenging obligations to manage, with cultural and familial expectations sometimes making saying "no" feel guilt-inducing. But remember you have an obligation to your well-being too - be polite yet firm when standing your ground, while remaining respectful throughout.

"No" should always be your default response in certain situations that involve your body and personal space, including consent agreements and sexual scenarios. Maintaining your autonomy requires standing firm when your boundaries are at stake - whether or not that involves sexual relationships.

Have you decided to utter that terrifying two-letter word? Afterward, your reaction may range from relief and guilt; both are normal reactions. Take some time to assess how emotionally and physically relaxed or anxious you feel as a result of making this choice; perhaps anxiously is related to fear of judgment?

Saying no is an art, requiring balance between your needs and those of others. Saying "no" regularly will become easier over time as your understanding of yourself and boundaries deepens.

So feel free to give it a try: the next time your gut tells you not to do something, heed its advice. Rather, this is about self-awareness rather than selfishness, with an important distinction between them both.

5.4 Becoming Adaptable to Change

We have all heard it a thousand times before - adaptability is our friend when dealing with change! Be it personal or professional life changes are inevitable: seasons shift, people change and so does everyone's own evolution - some changes happen gradually giving plenty of time for adjustment while others can come about suddenly and require swift responses - adaptability should always be your top priority when confronted by sudden shifts.

Change can come in various forms - both externally and internally. External changes include shifts in your environment such as job loss, moving to a different city or an abrupt breakup, while internal shifts may involve beliefs, attitudes or personal revelations that occur from within you. Being adaptive means successfully adapting to both types of change.

Change can be unnerving, yet inevitable. We get so comfortable with our daily lives that any disruption threatens our comfort zones, creating anxiety in us that must be overcome in order to face life as it comes. But mastering it requires resilience if we want to successfully face life head on!

Being adaptable does more than mean being adept at dealing with change - it also encompasses resilience, emotional intelligence and high stress tolerance. Being open to new experiences and ideas also fosters creativity - like having your own Swiss Army knife with multifaceted edges for anything life throws your way!

Neuroscientifically speaking, when exposed to change, your brain begins rewiring itself - this is known as neuroplasticity - forming new connections and pathways. That's pretty remarkable! Let's break it down further:

- Denial: You simply cannot believe this is happening;
- Anger: You feel angry because this situation exists;
- Bargaining: You look for ways around it;
- Depression: Feeling overwhelmed by all that change.
- Acceptance: Accept it and do what's necessary to adapt.

These stages don't follow a linear progression; you may skip some, move swiftly between them or experience them all at the same time - the key is reaching acceptance as quickly as possible for peace of mind.

Being adaptable doesn't mean losing yourself; in fact, it means expanding it and refining it with each change you experience - adding another facet of character that makes up who you are as an amazing individual.

- **Stay Curious:** Knowledge increases with age allowing us to better adapt ourselves.

- **Be Open-Minded:** Being flexible can open the door to new perspectives that offer unique solutions.

- **Develop Problem Solving Skills:** These will be essential tools in adapting.

- **Stay Positive:** A positive outlook goes a long way in making any transition smoother.

Setting boundaries and saying no are great, but what happens when an unexpected change crosses those boundaries? To adapt effectively to any new situation without compromising, adjust your boundaries as necessary - that way you don't compromise; you just adjust.

Life can be an unpredictable journey with its fair share of ups and downs and unexpected turns. Being adaptable won't make the ride any less unpredictable or exciting, but it will certainly enhance it! So the next time life throws you a curveball, don't duck: take aim, adapt, and throw back.

5.4.1 Embracing Uncertainty

Let's begin by acknowledging uncertainty as the elephant in the room. Uncertainty can be frightening because it's like walking through an unfamiliar dark room without a flashlight - you don't know what lies ahead and your mind might start filling in blanks with nightmare-inducing ideas that tap into deepest fears and insecurities, leading us down paths of self-doubt and doubt about competence or worth. So yes, uncertainty can be an enormously consequential issue

Uncertainty can arise in unexpected ways; sometimes even small events bring it. You might wonder whether your boss liked your presentation or what that cryptic text from a friend really means; uncertainty pervades all aspects of our relationships and lives - the sooner we recognize this fact, the better prepared we'll be to manage it effectively.

Do not misunderstand me; uncertainty has its own unique purpose and should not be dismissed outright as negative. Uncertainty serves both sides by raising anxiety and stress levels while providing an opportunity for growth, innovation, and discovery. Many great achievements were the product of uncertainty; consider life-altering inventions or magnificent pieces of artwork created during uncharted waters. Sometimes our curiosity compels us to dive deeper and seek new frontiers.

Viewing uncertainty through an optimistic lens is critical. If you see it as an enemy, fighting it and resisting will only compound your stress levels further. But by viewing uncertainty as a challenge to conquer instead, your emotional and psychological responses to uncertainty could change - this is where adaptability skills become invaluable!

Psychologists refer to this process as Cognitive Shifting; the process involves changing our thinking about something in an effort to reduce fear and uncertainty. Instead of dwelling on thoughts like "What if I'm not good enough?," shift your attention towards creating opportunities to learn and make an impactful contribution - small changes with big impacts!

Psychological flexibility means accepting both thoughts and emotions while taking steps that enrich your life. In times of uncertainty, this means acknowledging fears but letting them guide rather than control your decisions; saying: "Fear, I hear you, but you aren't the boss of me!"

Accepting uncertainty doesn't have to mean abandoning all rationality; taking an informed approach to risk can help smooth your transition into unfamiliar terrain. You should examine each scenario individually: what's the worst-case scenario; what could go right; and how can we mitigate risks by taking steps like these. Being rational can often make fears seem less intimidating and intimidating.

I love this one! Write down all the 'What If' scenarios that bug you. For instance, if you're uncertain about a new relationship, your list might look like:

- What if they don't like the real me?

- What if it doesn't work out?

- What if we can't resolve conflicts?

Once you have your list, try to think of solutions or positive outcomes for each 'What If.' You'll be surprised at how liberating it is to take control, even if it's just hypothetical at this point.

Accepting uncertainty can be challenging, and rationalizing won't completely alleviate emotional pain. But cultivating emotional resilience--your ability to rebound from hardship--can be life changing. Doing this means confronting fears head on, leaning into discomfort and emerging stronger from it all.

Remind yourself that you don't have to navigate this journey alone. Your tribe, squad or family can provide emotional support and practical advice when needed. Furthermore, discussing uncertainties with someone else may give new perspectives and make the unknown less intimidating.

Accepting uncertainty requires relinquishing control of all aspects of life - an illusion anyway; sooner we accept life's uncertainties the happier and more fulfilled our lives will become.

Uncertainty can be like an open book; embracing it opens doors for personal growth, enriching experiences and greater insight into yourself and the world. So when faced with uncertainty, take a deep breath, put on your bravest smile and step boldly into a great adventure!

5.4.2 Strategies for Easier Transitions

Before you dismiss mindfulness outright as just another mindfulness sermon, allow me to show you why it can make transitions much smoother. Mindfulness helps us focus on the present moment rather than looking ahead, which can be particularly powerful when approaching significant change. Mindfulness pulls back the stress from future-thinking and anxiety. How to practice? Try simple breathing exercises or 5-minute meditation sessions as ways back to reality - I guarantee they work every time!

Let's be real here; spontaneity can be enjoyable, but planning is necessary when transitioning through big life changes. Planning doesn't have to mean creating a detailed long-term blueprint, though. Setting achievable short-term goals and manageable to-dos will work just as well; think of it like having Google Maps for life: you know your destination and have an established path ahead of you that leads there.

Routines can be invaluable during times of transition. By creating small, manageable routines that you can adhere to easily - be it a morning walk or reading for 30 minutes before bed - they provide structure that offers control and normalcy when everything else feels unpredictable. By sticking with routines you create pockets of certainty in a world full of uncertainty.

At this stage, it's essential that you surround yourself with people who will support and comfort you through every phase of life. We often underestimate the power of venting sessions or the comforting words from someone we trust - keep this person close during times of transition so they can act as your emotional anchor when feeling lost or confused.

Life isn't a sprint; it's a marathon. To keep yourself going during transitional periods, celebrate small victories along the way - landing an interview for that job you want is a victory; speaking up about an issue with someone is another major win; these small achievements can serve as powerful morale boosters and make long-term goals seem more achievable.

Setbacks are part of life, so why let them get you down? What matters is how you respond when they occur; resilience is what enables us to rebound quickly from setbacks, take them in stride, and keep moving forward despite them. One timeless trick for resilience is viewing setbacks not as failures but rather learning opportunities - this method always proves successful.

So you have planned, established routines, and built your support system - but when things don't go according to plan? Flexibility comes into play here: the ability to adapt quickly to new situations and reconfigure plans when transitions arise is a vital asset during times of change. Just like being an excellent improv actor: just take whatever comes your way and make it work; there's never too late to change strategies!

Transitions don't just involve external changes; they also come with an emotional rollercoaster ride. One day you might feel excited for what lies ahead; then the next moment it could leave you grappling with nostalgia or fear - that's normal! Acknowledging these feelings without judgment will often help lessen their impact and lessen anxiety levels.

Transitions often necessitate new or enhanced capabilities. From career changes that necessitate technical abilities to lifestyle shifts that necessitate better time management skills, using this period as an opportunity to acquire additional abilities is a smart strategy; you won't simply adapt to change; you're using it for personal growth!

As I understand it, sometimes no matter the preparation and emotional groundwork done to prepare for transitions, things just don't pan out as anticipated. Knowing when it is necessary to move on is just as essential in successfully managing transitions as any other strategy; no shame should come with making that choice, rather it becomes an invaluable life lesson that sets up for future success.

5.5 Cultivating a Growth Mindset

Still confused? Allow me to shed some light. Carol Dweck first introduced this term, which describes believing you can improve and grow through dedication and hard work - the antidote for "fixed mindset," the belief that you have limited intellect or talent which may only exist at birth. With a growth mindset, the world truly is your oyster!

Let's assume you're terrible at math; seriously terrible; still counting on fingers and dreading splitting the bill at dinner. A fixed mindset would say, "I just am not good at math and never will be," while a growth mindset challenges you to think differently by challenging you to consider that "I may not be great yet, but with practice I can become better." Notice the difference? "Yet" opens a world of opportunities.

Your brain is like a muscle: the more you use it, the stronger it gets. Every time you challenge yourself by pushing past comfort zones or facing challenges that stretch mental muscles, new neural pathways are created; just like lifting weights at a gym builds physical muscle. Each time you push past comfort zones or face challenges you are literally becoming smarter through science!

As far as mindset goes, this one is hugely consequential. People in a fixed mindset world worship ability; those who come naturally adept at something are hero-worshiped. On the flipside of that coin: If something comes difficult for you, a fixed mindset can make you feel inadequate and make life seem hopeless. Enter growth mindset: its focus shifts away from ability toward effort: rather than measuring how good someone already is at something; its aim is not about how long and hard people are willing to put in until they master it!

Life will always throw you curveballs; that's just part of life's game. With a growth mindset, challenges don't need to be barriers; they're opportunities for greatness! Don't shrink back from them but step up to them; embrace them like old friends coming into make you stronger, wiser, and more resilient - and welcome new experiences with an open heart and mind - the growth mindset helps us see obstacles as opportunities that expand horizons!

When you find yourself stuck, unsure if progress is being made, add the word 'yet' to any negative thought about yourself or something you do not excel in. "I am not good at this" can become "I am not good at this, yet." This provides room to grow while reminding yourself that each challenge provides opportunities for personal development.

At first blush, no one enjoys criticism - it stings, bruises our ego and can leave us reeling in pain. But take a step back: In a growth mindset, constructive criticism should not be taken personally but seen as a gift - someone taking time out of their day to point out where improvement needs to occur is truly valued and should not be dismissed outright as criticism; just take note. Of course this doesn't mean agreeing with every piece of feedback but at least consider each one; if it applies, use it and improve; otherwise let go but don't let it weigh you down either!

If you find yourself thinking, "This sounds wonderful, but I'm too set in my ways," stop right there. One of the great aspects of having a growth mindset is its non-age-specificity; whether you are 15 or 50, there's never too late to adopt one and improve yourself! Your brain can still learn and adapt; why put an expiration date on self-improvement?

5.5.1 Fixed vs. Growth Mindset

Oh, that age-old battle: Fixed Mindset versus Growth Mindset. Imagine these two protagonists as heroes from a superhero film; on one side is the Fixed Mindset, filled with doubt about change or growth; while the Growth Mindset boasts optimism, resilience, and an eagerness for learning. Who do you think will emerge victorious over time? Let's dig deeper and find out.

Before we cast Fixed Mindset as the ultimate villain, let's give it its due. Sometimes it serves a protective function: for instance, if you believe you lack ability in something, your Fixed Mindset may shield you from situations that might embarrass or shame you; think of it like your mind's risk management committee! But that also prevents opportunities to learn, grow, and excel; so while not entirely bad or good at times; think of it like that sketchy friend who offers support without actually helping to push forward your goals in life!

Let's consider some of the drawbacks. When operating from a fixed mindset, failure feels like an identity crisis. Didn't get that job? Embark upon an unfamiliar task without success and you might believe yourself incapable - every setback seems like a life sentence telling you, "You aren't good enough!" What an unbearable burden!

Growth Mindset can be your hero. This mindset gives you the tools to turn failure into feedback and transform each hiccup into an opportunity for personal development. So when you slip up, rather than becoming mired in self-doubt and self-sabotage, look at it as an opportunity for progress on an improved path - embrace every bump and scrape as an experience that helps form you into a wiser, more resilient individual.

Once you genuinely believe you can grow, it creates the conditions for it to happen. Your mind responds by saying: "Okay, let's do this." And this isn't just fluffy feel-good talk; studies have proven that students taught principles of growth mindset saw improvements in grades. Additionally, workplaces that adopted growth mindset cultures reported higher employee engagement and productivity - so this strategy delivers real results!

Think you're too entrenched in Team Fixed Mindset to switch sides? Think again. Although your mindset may have formed through early life experiences, it doesn't need to remain static over time. The first step to changing is awareness: recognize when Fixed Mindset triggers arise so you can actively choose how you respond using Growth Mindset approaches instead.

Let us not underestimate the power of words here. How you use language has an immense effect on shaping your mindset. Fixed mindset statements tend to be definitive such as, "I can't do this," while growth mindset statements could include something like: "I can't yet" or "I need another approach". Small changes to internal dialogue could result in tremendous shifts in your perspective.

No one is 100% either fixed or growth mindsets; we all possess both. That's perfectly fine; having some degree of both in our mindsets may keep us grounded from time to time; the key is making sure your growth mindset is the driving force in all your choices and pushing you toward constructive development, change, and living a good life.

5.5.2 Cultivating Curiosity

Now is the time to prepare! We're taking a deep dive into something that could very well be the essence of a Growth Mindset: Curiosity. If Growth Mindset were a tree, curiosity would provide the water needed for its roots to expand further while its leaves gain light from sunlight, giving it life - all while feeding into an endless cycle. But perhaps more practically? After discussing Fixed vs Growth Mindsets and exploring their respective advantages and disadvantages, let's discover how curiosity could act as your ultimate superpower and explore its capabilities! Curiosity can do wonders for our lives - let us explore!

Let's be clear about this from the outset: curiosity is not something you need to 'install' into your system like some newfangled app; it was already there when you were born! Just think back to when your toddler self would always ask "why" or touch things just to see how they felt, always eager for exploring... That was your true curiosity at work! Over time, however, that questioning may have faded, yet that spirit remains; let's awaken it!

Imagine this. Alice and Bob enroll in a cooking class. Alice has long been fascinated with culinary arts and she wonders at how spices blend, heat changes texture and the end result can bring joy. Bob on the other hand simply wants to add another skill to his resume. Who do you think will gain more from their class? Curiosity will play a huge role - Alice will find the process engaging while Bob may simply use it as another means of adding value to their resume. Research supports curiosity-driven learning as an excellent method of memory retention! So it really is a win-win situation!

Imagine this: you have a problem that's been plaguing you, like an impenetrable riddle you just can't solve. Instead of viewing it as an impediment (a classic Fixed Mindset move), why not approach it with curiosity instead? Asking questions such as, "What can I learn from this?" and "How can I approach this from different angles?" can turn any situation into something worthwhile to solve - rather than an obstacle standing in your way! Engaging curiosity makes any challenge look less like something to overcome but rather something you must engage with to bring about positive change that ultimately affects outcomes and approaches alike! It could make all the difference to how we approach problems and ultimately, results.

Curiosity can do amazing things for relationships. Instead of labeling people or jumping to conclusions, why don't we try being curious instead of labeling? Next time someone annoys or puzzles you, instead of rolling your eyes or becoming annoyed, instead try being curious instead and try understanding their point of view instead - you might just discover an entirely new level of empathy or understanding with those whom previously seemed irritating - who knows, your biggest pet peeve may turn out to be something truly admirable once we understand why!

Fear may be holding you back, but what if we changed that into curiosity instead? Instead of fearing what's unknown, explore it - then magic happens; fear no longer paralyzes;

curiosity propels. Imagine all the doors that would open if only just one step was taken towards curiosity instead!

Now you understand the why of curiosity, but how can you actively cultivate it in daily life? Mindfulness. Be present in each moment; engage your senses when taking a walk - feel the breeze, listen for leaves rustling underfoot and observe colors around you; make it an interactive sensory experience! And ask lots of questions; start within yourself then expand to examine global issues; challenge beliefs and preconceptions while probing deeper for answers to underlying principles rather than simply accepting easy solutions as answers.

Let me conclude this discussion by emphasizing that curiosity is an ongoing journey; not an event to experience once and be done with. Your questions might change over time as your life develops - that's okay; just remember to keep asking, exploring, and growing with curiosity as your guide on this incredible hike called life! Curiosity should lead the way on an incredible adventure; let it guide your steps as each step brings new insights while opening up more questions - that keeps the journey enjoyable and stimulating!

Part 6: Making Improvements at Work

6.1 Work-Life Balance

By now we've dived deep into your emotions, self-esteem, and mindset - but there is another dimension we should discuss: your job. Sure, work occupies much of our waking hours but that does not define all aspects of our lives; let's explore ways we can strike a balance between professional endeavors and personal ones, shall we?

Let's first dispel a myth. Attempts at striking an ideal "work-life balance," where hours are evenly allocated among work, family, friends, self-care and hobbies are like looking for unicorns: beautiful in theory but impossible in practice. Life's unpredictable and changing dynamics mean the balance won't ever be 50-50: there will be days, weeks or even months where work demands more from you and other times when personal life needs priority - the key here is adaptability and going with the flow!

Work-life balance is often defined in terms of time. But don't overlook energy - just eight hours spent working at one job may drain all your life away, thus rendering any type of balance impossible to attain. Even during family time you could still be mentally focused on work by planning presentations or replying to emails; thus rendering those precious hours spent together without real connections not worth much!

Imagine this: your life is like a jigsaw puzzle with various roles--employee, parent, partner, friend and self--being filled in one piece at a time. Instead, focus on one role at a time:

today it may be an all-star employee to complete a project; tomorrow could mean being an outstanding parent at your kid's soccer match; over the weekend how about wearing yourself' hat by getting involved in something you are passionate about or taking time for yourself?

No two people's work-life balance needs are identical. Your friend who prefers four days might not share your same responsibilities and obligations, and vice versa; similarly, colleagues who make 6 am gym classes a must may have different priorities than you. Don't get caught in comparison traps: define what balance means to you and strive to achieve it.

Setting boundaries is central to finding that all-elusive balance. Applying the same principles we discussed for interpersonal relationships applies here; you must define your professional life's limits to make room for your personal life - such as turning off emails after certain hours or setting aside weekends for 'prime-time' or family bonding time. Emails can wait; your mental wellbeing cannot.

An often-overlooked aspect of work-life balance is transition time. How you switch gears can have a major effect on both, particularly if you work from home - setting aside 10 minutes for meditation or changing into loungewear can help signal to your brain that work has ended and let go of its hold on you.

Let's be clear. Achieving work-life balance is not solely your responsibility - employers play an integral role too. A culture that supports balance, flexibility, and well-being will facilitate an ideal working-life dynamic. If possible, advocate for these policies; otherwise selecting an employer who values balance makes its own statement.

Living in an age where everyone is always available can be both beneficial and detrimental, depending on how it's used. Technology can blur the lines between work and personal life, making it hard to switch off, yet at other times allowing greater balance through working from anywhere - it all depends on how we use this double-edged sword!

Work and life often battle it out in an epic struggle that leads to sacrifices in social life. Social activities, whether that means hanging out with friends, attending social events, or just relaxing with your partner may take second place; yet these activities help rejuvenate you, making all other roles easier to fulfill. Take time out for social activities - they aren't time wasted; rather an investment in your well-being!

Finally, work-life balance should not be an 'end of story' scenario. Priorities and the world at large will change over time - just look around you! So it is essential that you regularly assess yourself: is your current routine fulfilling its purpose and if not what needs tweaking? Balance is about maintaining equilibrium as life experiences its highs and lows.

6.1.1 Finding Your Sweet Spot

Before we jump in, it is essential that we are clear on the definition of our target goal of finding our "sweet spot." To do this, imagine two circles; one represents work commitments while the other represents personal life responsibilities; where they overlap without collapsing into each other is where your "sweet spot" resides - it's where productivity meets peace, duties meet dreams, and where you can be your most authentic self.

Let's disprove another myth here. Your sweet spot doesn't involve attaining perfection in both work and life - that goal is both unattainable and an immense waste of your energy. Instead, optimizer is far more rewarding; optimization means aligning actions with values dynamically - much like how a car runs best when properly tuned - your life requires regular tweaks to stay on course smoothly.

Finding your sweet spot begins with developing an in-depth knowledge of yourself - your values, priorities, limitations and even any quirks that make you unique. If family is your top priority then your sweet spot should focus on providing quality time with loved ones. If professional growth is your focus then your ideal situation might include dedicated time for skill building outside regular working hours. No one else can determine where or how you find your sweet spot; it is an individual quest.

Now that you have established a set of values, let's not let them fester in the back of our minds. Your values should serve as your compass in everyday decisions and actions - any work commitment that conflicts with a core value should set off an internal alarm bell; when actions line up with values more consistently, the closer we come to finding our personal sweet spot.

Create a Time vs. Value Matrix to bring greater clarity: this simple exercise could bring great insight. List how you spend your time at work and elsewhere on one axis; rate the value or satisfaction you derive from each activity on the other side; this will allow you to identify time sinks - those activities which occupy significant time but offer limited or no value in return. Once identified, reduce or eliminate them to make room for more fulfilling activities.

News flash: Your sweet spot isn't set in stone; it's more like sketched in sand. As life throws you a curveball, your equilibrium may shift as well; don't become rigid; adapt and adjust in order to find new equilibrium whenever life presents you with new obstacles. Bruce Lee would advise us not to be rigid but "be like water". When challenges come your way, find new equilibrium by being fluid and adaptable!

Boundaries are essential in finding your sweet spot, whether that means setting hard stops on workdays, carving out some weekly me-time, or communicating openly with boss and family about what realistic goals can be accomplished. Once boundaries have been set up, respect them as sacred - no cheating!

So how do you know when you're hitting this intangible sweet spot? You'll feel it, but let's quantify it a bit:

- You'll start each day with a sense of purpose.

- Stress will be present but manageable.

- You'll be achieving your goals without feeling like you're running a never-ending marathon.

- You'll have time for yourself and your loved ones, and it won't feel like a juggling act.

- You'll feel fulfilled, not just 'busy.'

While it might sound cliche, finding your sweet spot can be equally enriching as reaching it. The journey will teach you much about yourself - your strengths, weaknesses, desires - as well as make you appreciate any difficulties on the way - they provide opportunities to fine-tune that sweet spot of yours!

Once you find your sweet spot, the temptation will be strong to rest on your laurels and become complacent. Unfortunately, complacency is the enemy of growth, so keep pushing yourself to set new goals and move out of your comfort zone a bit at a time. Think of upgrading to a new software version; once experiencing all its new features you realize some old bugs were holding you back before.

Your sweet spot lies at the intersection of work and personal goals, not in having to choose between the two; it's about integration. Think of your life as being your canvas - your work goals and personal goals represent different hues on a palette that come together on canvas as artfully blended masterpieces.

No discussion of finding our sweet spot would be complete without acknowledging all of the factors that shape it - externally these could include work environment expectations, boss's demands or social norms while internally they could include mental health, physical stamina or emotional resilience. The key here is not letting these influences define where your sweet spot lies but using them as guides on your journey toward it.

Simply stated: Your sweet spot is all about you. It represents the decisions, victories and setbacks in your life that reflect who you truly are - so own them, learn from them and strive to align them with who you really are in order to find your sweet spot and live life on your terms.

6.1.2 Balancing Family and Career

It can be challenging balancing family life with professional obligations. On one side are quarterly reports, deadlines, meetings, and performance reviews; on the other are your partner's important work event, child recital performance rehearsal, family outings, bedtime stories that cannot be replaced, bedtime stories. Yikes! Sounds daunting? But we have this topic under control; together we will find ways to keep that tightrope from becoming an imminent tripwire!

Let's address one misconception first and foremost: the notion of having it all. This phrase often heard in self-help books and motivational seminars sets unrealistic expectations by suggesting there is some magical formula where all elements fall into place seamlessly - when in reality there are only choices and tradeoffs - and that's perfectly acceptable: having what matters most to you should always be your goal, not having it all!

Debunking myths, here is another pointer--every choice has an associated cost, or trade-off. When opting for full throttle career aspirations you might need to sacrifice quality time with family, while being dedicated solely to family may force you to give up some career aspirations. Recognizing these trade-offs is the first step towards finding balance; once aware, informed choices can be made that help meet long-term goals.

Your life can be thought of like a jar, with rocks, pebbles and sand needing to fill every crevice of space in it. Here is how this metaphor applies in practice: rocks represent your major priorities like family and health care needs while pebbles represent smaller but still significant items like hobbies or social circles; finally sand represents distractions like television viewing or scrolling social media feeds. To maintain balance it's key that we prioritize big issues first: pebbles can fill gaps as needed but without prioritizing big stuff first jar will become overfull with no balance possible!

Goal setting is like Google Maps for your life: just input your destination and it outlines a route. However, to achieve success with goal setting it is crucial that realistic, attainable goals be set for both family and career - setting unrealistic ones is like asking Google Maps to get you from New York to London by car; unrealistic goals don't work! Your goals should stretch you without breaking you and be achievable - after all a wish without an action plan is just that-a wish!

Time management doesn't mean cramming more tasks into your day; rather, it means prioritizing what truly matters. That may mean saying no to opportunities that don't align with your larger goals even if they appear attractive; consider your time as your most precious commodity--spend it wisely both professionally and personally!

Ever find yourself attending a meeting while your mind wanders off into dinner planning or, conversely, planning for a presentation? That is not true balance; that is being physically present but mentally absent. Achieve true equilibrium by being fully present wherever you are: when with family be with them wholeheartedly while when at work give everything your all.

Guilt can be an unproductive emotion that rears its ugly head anytime we feel as if we're not doing 'enough' in one or more aspects of life. Yet guilt should not be the driving force in your decision making - do the best you can with what circumstances allow and don't waste energy dwelling on unfounded feelings of shame; change what can be and accept what can't.

Flexibility is your greatest ally when it comes to managing family and career obligations simultaneously. Sometimes your family needs you more, sometimes your work does, so being rigidly committed to either can prove disastrous for achieving balance. Allow yourself the flexibility of missing minor work deadlines when your child becomes sick, or postponing family movie night when something major arises requiring your focus.

Buffer zones are those special moments you intentionally set aside to transition between work and family or vice versa, be it through physical exercise, meditation sessions, or simply changing out of work clothes. By creating these buffer zones you allow your brain to switch gears so you can be fully present for the next part of the day.

If you find it difficult to strike a balance, don't keep it all to yourself. Speak out about your struggles with family members or employers as soon as you notice any imbalance; open dialogue could lead to shared solutions and reduced burdens.

Technology, while extremely beneficial, can blur the line between work and home life. So make it a practice to 'unplug' when spending quality time with loved ones - emails or Slack messages don't need answering just yet; unplugging helps establish clear boundaries while safeguarding quality time with family.

Keep in mind that living a balanced life includes taking some time for just you. Be it hobbies, exercising, reading or doing nothing at all - "me time" is essential in rejuvenating and becoming more effective both at work and home; plus happier individuals often make for happier family or work environments!

Last but certainly not least, let go of the illusion that you need to excel in every aspect at all times - that can be a trap! Striving for excellence is good; obsessing over perfection is mental quicksand. Allow yourself the grace of just being "good enough", remembering that balance is not an endpoint but an ongoing journey.

Now, to really drive home these points, create a collage depicting these elements -- such as pictures of rocks and jars for the "Rocks, Pebbles, Sand" analogy or an image of a tightrope walker to symbolize how to balance family with career goals. Visual aids can serve as powerful reminders that make this learning journey even more impactful.

6.2 Stress Management at Work

Now let's address one of the biggest topics on our agenda-- stress management in the workplace. Stress can be that unwelcome guest who crashes your otherwise well-planned party; but here's the good news: while it won't go away completely (let's be realistic here), we can certainly find ways to manage it better and help each other navigate our way through this labyrinth of workplace tension together.

Before we set forth on our stress-busting adventure, let's pause to consider why stress arises in the workplace. For several reasons, including unrealistic deadlines, competing priorities, and ever-evolving team dynamics; workplace stressors include unrealistic deadlines, conflicting priorities and poor leadership - making for a stress cocktail no one requested yet everyone is forced to drink!

Did you know stress isn't only ruining your mind; it's wreaking havoc on your body as well? Stress triggers what's known as the "fight or flight" response, sending stress hormones like cortisol rushing through your system like crazy when faced with real danger - perfect when running from saber-toothed tigers - but less desirable when just sitting at a desk all day long. Long term chronic stress exposure has been linked with high blood pressure, insomnia and even heart conditions - both health issues which require professional medical help when dealing with.

Stress has no place in job performance either, however. Being stressed tends to narrow your focus and cause you to miss vital details; like wearing blinders; you only see what's right in front of you. Plus, stress often leads to burnout--that feeling of complete mental, emotional and physical exhaustion which makes even simple tasks seem herculean and productivity plummet.

Now that we've discussed the issue, how about some solutions? One word will do: mindfulness. You may have heard this word used frequently recently; there's good reason for its widespread popularity: Mindfulness means being fully present without overreacting. When feeling overwhelmed, take some time out for breathing exercises or simply observe your thoughts without judgment - you'll be amazed how this simple act will ground you back into the present moment!

But that doesn't have to be a problem! Microbreaks offer you a solution: short 30-second to 2-minute breaks where you simply take a quick look away from your computer screen, stretch a bit, maybe walk around your workspace, and look away for at least 30-seconds or two minutes. Think of microbreaks as mini reboots for your mind that break the monotony while refreshing it!

Eisenhower Matrix is another useful tool that will help you decide and prioritize tasks by categorizing them as urgent, important, urgent but unimportant and neither urgent nor important. By organizing tasks this way, it ensures you're not simply fighting fires all day but are instead planning long-term strategies, thus decreasing stress levels.

If you tend to take on too much and assume you can handle everything on your own, now may be the time for a wake-up call. Delegating does not indicate weakness; rather it demonstrates smart time and stress management. Delegate tasks that do not require your specific expertise to team members who can perform them more effectively; not only will this relieve your workload but it will also empower them and create an inclusive team atmosphere - two birds with one stone!

Negative thinking can be devastating for stress management, fueling endless worry and worsening any existing tension. Recognize negative thought patterns early and address them immediately with positive affirmations or, at minimum, neutral observations; try replacing your negative thoughts with something like: This task may seem impossible but by breaking it into smaller tasks and approaching it step-by-step I can manage to complete it successfully."

Never underestimate the impact of your physical environment on your mental state. A cluttered workspace can contribute to stress. Take some time at the end of each day to declutter. Add personal touches such as plants or pictures that bring joy - these small steps will create an oasis where stress won't thrive as readily.

Have you heard of the Pomodoro Technique? This system involves working in bursts of intense focus for approximately 25 minutes at a time, followed by short 5-minute breaks to keep your mind sharp and fresh - ideal for managing multiple tasks without feeling overwhelmed! Give it a try; you might just discover its productivity benefits!

Don't try to be perfect all of the time; you are human after all, and mistakes happen. By relinquishing the need to be perfect, a significant burden is lifted off of your shoulders, along with much-needed relief of stress.

Physical exercise is a proven stress reliever. Even taking a quick 10-minute stroll around your neighborhood can do wonders to clear your head. Exercising releases endorphins

- nature's feel-good chemicals which work as natural stress relief agents - and acts like natural antidotes.

Last but certainly not least, manage both your own expectations and those of others. Be clear on what can realistically be accomplished within any given timeframe; overcommitting is the surest path to stress.

6.2.1 Identifying Workplace Triggers

We often hear the term 'trigger' thrown around without much clarity as to what it really means. A stress trigger refers to any situation, person, or thought which causes stress for you; for example it could be anything from an overwhelming mountain of emails waiting for your attention or someone's attempts at disrupting your daily work routine. Identifying these specific triggers might feel tedious but is the first step on the journey towards stress-free nirvana.

One way to identify hidden stressors in your workday is through conducting an audit. One approach is keeping a stress diary; though it might seem high schoolish, this approach works - just jot down moments when you feel stressed out and what might have caused it; was it that two p.m. meeting that always drags on? Was it all those emails clogging your inboxes at once? Recording everything allows an outside perspective that helps reveal patterns you might otherwise miss.

So let's focus on specific triggers, starting with emails. A stream of unending messages flooding into your inbox can feel like quicksand - especially if its quality or quantity irks you; sometimes its not the quantity but its tone that drives us crazy; is it your manager's vague instructions, or those passive-aggressive comments masquerading as feedback that are driving you crazy? By pinpointing aspects of emails that stress you out, strategies can be created to mitigate their effect; maybe allocating specific times to check them, or communicating directly with those sending it directly about their concerns.

Next up is something I call 'Phantom Deadline Syndrome'-- those looming deadlines that appear seemingly out of nowhere. If this is your Achilles Heel, make a plan using digital calendars for planners (even old school Post-its can work!), milestones and buffer periods so as not to add even more stress! Planning will save the day!

Let's focus on the human element. Co-workers, managers and clients all play an integral part in workplace dynamics - and not always for the better. Are you feeling stressed over your relationship with certain co-workers or clients? Is their behavior or your reaction to their behavior leaving you second-guessing and stressed? Perhaps lack of clear communication has left you confused and stressed out; or perhaps its not even them at all; sometimes it's about how we let their actions impact us; once this issue is addressed you can work on conflict-resolution techniques, assertiveness training or improving communication channels to establish better workplace dynamics and communication channels for all parties involved.

Lacking autonomy? Feeling trapped? A lack of autonomy can be an intense source of anxiety for many; without control over tasks, timing, or workspace it can feel like constantly treading carefully. If this applies to you, consider having an open dialogue with your manager about taking steps towards more control in the workplace - even small adjustments could bring significant relief; otherwise perhaps it's time to reconsider whether your current role fits with your values and needs.

Work-life imbalance is another major concern. If you find yourself working late and thinking about work during "off hours", that should be an alarm bell for you. Your job shouldn't overshadow other aspects of life like family, friends, and hobbies; such an imbalance could create unnecessary stress while potentially leading to burnout. Setting clear boundaries between personal time and professional obligations is critical for emotional and physical well-being.

Role ambiguity can also contribute to stress. Not knowing what's expected of you or constantly shifting expectations is a surefire way to feel overwhelmed and discomfited in your job - constantly worrying that something may be amiss with what's expected of you. Clear communication with your manager can work wonders here: set tangible goals and deadlines together so everyone understands what they should expect of each other.

Companies change, it's inevitable. How you are communicated and implemented these changes can have a major effect on your stress levels. If your company is going through a merger, restructuring, or simply updating its basic operational software changes can be extremely stressful; keeping in the know can reduce this anxiety; don't be shy to ask questions and get clarity if something seems amiss!

Perfectionism can be an entrapping double-edged sword: on one side it drives you to produce stellar work; but on the other it sets off stress bombs. Setting your standard of success at nothing less than perfection sets yourself up for disappointment and anxiety-inducing stress levels to soar. Learning to embrace "good enough" may seem counterintuitive to your work ethic but trust me - it will liberate you.

Let's not forget job security and future uncertainties either. Even in relatively secure jobs, the unpredictable economic landscape can leave one feeling uneasy about their future prospects. While being prepared for changes is essential, dwelling on potential outcomes only adds unnecessary anxiety to an already stressful situation.

6.2.2 Quick Stress-Busters for the Office

Now we understand what's triggering you at work. Knowledge is power, but quick solutions may be needed immediately while developing long-term plans. So buckle up; here we go; here are quick stress-busters you can incorporate into daily office life to quickly relieve tension - trust me; these could be game-changers!

So here's the thing: your mind and body are intimately interlinked, so when your mental state becomes chaotic, your physical wellbeing also takes a hit. Enter the five-minute breather: an easy technique designed to give an overloaded brain some relief. Find a quiet corner, close your eyes, take deep breaths inward and outward and imagine that each exhale pushes away stress as it comes. Even if office spaces can be noisy, putting on noise-canceling headphones can help provide this quick refreshment for both minds. This quick refreshment can provide a mini reboot for the mind as soon as a five minute breather provides mental rejuvenation for both mind and body!

Yoga mats and office chairs may seem worlds apart, but hear me out: desk yoga is real and not as weird as you might think! Simple stretches can do wonders to relieve tension in your neck, shoulders and back - often the first places that stress impacts our health. Twist your torso, roll your shoulders or stretch arms - even small movements like twisting can boost energy levels while simultaneously decreasing stress! Give seated warriors a try without worry that other workers might take offense!

Visuals can be powerful tools in combating stress. I don't mean vision boards or inspirational quotes here - though these may help, too; rather I mean taking a mental trip to your happy place. When your stress levels escalate, close your eyes for a minute and visualize yourself somewhere peaceful - whether that be on a beach, forest or your grandmother's kitchen; the goal here should be complete immersion so that it almost feels like being there - almost feeling the sand between your toes or smelling those cookies bake while visualizing positive scenarios can help shift away from where that comes from by drawing your mind away from thinking about where that stress comes from and onto happier thoughts instead.

Yes, snacking can be an art. When we're stressed, our natural instincts often include reaching for comfort foods rich in sugar or salt that provide temporary mood-lifting before rapidly dissipating again. Instead of turning to unhealthy comfort food solutions like refined carbohydrates or sugary drinks for relief, consider keeping healthy snacks such as fruit, nuts or yogurt close at hand as these contain omega-3 fatty acids and Vitamin C that have proven stress-reducers effects - plus munching itself can act as a form of relaxation!

Movement can be an incredible stress reliever. Walking not only gets your legs moving but can help clear away mental cobwebs as well. A five-minute stroll around your office or outside in fresh air may do wonders to ease stress levels quickly and effectively; providing fresh air, change of scene, physical activity, and time out from a stressful environment all serve as effective rejuvenators.

Social support is a valuable weapon against stress. Sharing experiences with loved ones or talking things out with a trusted confidante for even just five minutes can offer invaluable relief and new perspective on things. Chit-chatting about trivial matters or anything that comes up can often do the trick; just remember not to procrastinate or postpone responsibility - take a brief respite so you can return with renewed vigor to your tasks!

"A cluttered desk can lead to an equally disorganized mind", as they say. Dedicating even just five minutes to tidying your workspace can give you a sense of control and accomplishment; file away papers that have fallen onto your desk, wipe down surfaces or rearrange pens -- these seemingly minor tasks may provide enough mental relief to lower stress levels.

Your plate may seem full, and that can be daunting. Enter the "two-minute rule" - a time management technique which encourages doing tasks that take less than two minutes immediately instead of leaving them accumulating until later on and becoming an added source of stress. Doing it this way prevents small tasks from piling up and becoming significant sources of worry later, while simultaneously giving a sense of accomplishment and inspiring you to tackle more significant tasks!

They say laughter is the best medicine and this certainly holds true when it comes to stress relief. Watching funny videos, reading comics or sharing a joke with colleagues can immediately lighten your mood and ease anxiety almost instantly. Involvement with laughing releases endorphins which act like natural painkillers within our bodies - so find something humorous that tickles your funny bone - it's doctor approved!

This technique may sound complex, but it's surprisingly straightforward. Simply tighten muscles as you breathe in and then relax them as you breathe out; do this step-by-step up from your toes until your entire body relaxes as it progresses upwards - no one needs to know! Doing this at your desk without drawing unnecessary attention will allow for effective release from physical tension.

Music can have an enormously healing effect on us emotionally, and finding songs or tracks that uplift you can turn any day around. Compose a playlist of soothing tracks or ones that lift your spirit; when stress begins to build up just plug in those headphones and let the melodies wash over you - the point here isn't to drown out all your troubles but rather to give yourself some respite so you're better equipped to deal with them later on.

Speak briefly of the benefits of unplugging. We become so dependent on digital devices that it's easy to forget they can be sources of stress. Notifications, emails and messages all demand our attention and can add significantly to stress levels. Try disconnecting for just a few minutes by setting your phone on Do Not Disturb or taking some time away from the computer; use this time either practicing any of the stress-busting strategies mentioned here, or just relaxing and enjoy being temporarily unreachable!

Now you have some quick stress-busters for the office! While these might not address the source of your distress directly, they can give you much-needed breathing space while painkillers take effect - like applying a cool compress during that wait time! These techniques can help recalibrate yourself so you can return into work more focused with spirits lifted and stress levels down. Choose one or two to experiment with and find your go-to quick stress-busting routine; I know you've got this!

6.3 Effective Communication Skills

Communication skills are an indispensable asset in professional and personal settings alike, but especially the workplace. Poor communication is at the root of many workplace issues such as conflict, miscommunication and inefficiencies; this chapter serves as a full guide on becoming an effective communicator at work! So make sure you buckle up; we're diving deep!

Let's start off by discussing verbal communication. Most of us take for granted our ability to talk, having been doing it since toddlerhood; but effective verbal communication requires much more than stringing together words - it requires being clear, concise, and focused in your approach - avoid using jargon unless 100% sure the other person understands; use simple language that gets directly to the point; time is often of the essence in a workplace environment!

Listening is an integral component of communication; just as important as speaking. Active listening involves truly hearing what the other person is saying, interpreting their meaning, and responding thoughtfully - not simply waiting your turn or anticipating counterarguments. Active listening makes speakers feel valued and heard - something everyone deserves! So next time someone speaks with you, use all five senses and truly listen!

Ever hear the phrase, "Actions speak louder than words"? Well, in terms of communication this statement holds true: nonverbal cues such as body language, gestures and facial expressions often convey messages more effectively than spoken language alone. A simple nod may show understanding; raising an eyebrow could indicate doubt; keeping steady eye contact can show confidence and attentiveness - however don't turn it into a staring contest which could become disconcerting!

Remote work has increased substantially, prompting us to explore virtual communication. Emails, video calls and chat apps all present unique challenges; physical cues can often cause misinterpretations while words don't carry any tone (unless using emojis) so be extra wary when communicating virtually - follow-up phone calls and video chats can often help clear things up quickly.

Emails are the cornerstone of office communication. However, writing effective emails requires careful thought. A strong subject line that attracts reader attention while accurately representing its content should be your starting point; then keep the email body succinct - no one likes reading a novel when short stories will do; bullet points can help break up complex data easily; finally don't forget to attach any necessary files before hitting send; that way no one needs to send follow up messages after realizing you forgot an attachment was necessary!

No one enjoys being criticized, but constructive criticism can be the foundation for great growth and improvement. Learning how to accept constructive feedback - truly absorb it and not simply nod in agreement- is a skill in itself; when someone offers up constructive advice or feedback for you, take note. Listen carefully before thanking them and using the information as an opportunity for growth and development.

There's an art to voicing your grievances or concerns at work without airing them out like dirty laundry. Approach the person involved at an appropriate time and setting, select an open yet focused discussion topic, and initiate contact via appropriate channels in your organization if it involves bigger issues that need escalating. Documenting concerns often helps your voice be heard.

Some may perceive small talk as an inconsequential aspect of workplace communication, but that would be inaccurate. These seemingly harmless conversations by the water cooler can provide the foundation for deeper, more meaningful relationships later. Who knows? You could learn something useful or gain a fresh outlook on an assignment!

Effective communication involves more than simply what we say - timing can make or break its impact. Avoid dropping bombshells near the end of each workday, and read your audience before speaking up in meetings; trust me, they'll thank you later!

Always bear in mind that communication isn't one-size-fits-all. People come with various communication styles, preferences and cultural backgrounds - what works well with one person may fall flat when communicating with someone else. Be observant and adaptable by tailoring your approach according to who is speaking with you - it's like matchmaking but for words and ideas!

6.3.1 Active Listening

Do you think of yourself as a good listener? Most of us do! Let's put that to the test; today we will explore active listening in depth--an invaluable skill which, as it turns out, can make or break careers - not only at work but in relationships and friendships as well. If listening seems ordinary or insignificant to you now, keep reading - today will reveal why it matters more than ever!

Let's first clarify what listening and active listening mean: passively taking in information such as television programs or gossip from friends while you decide what's for dinner, while actively listening is much different: deliberate, focused listening that involves not just hearing words but taking them in, dissecting them into meaning, and responding thoughtfully. Have we covered these differences sufficiently? Great; now let's see why active listening matters so much.

Your question might be: "So what if I listen actively or passively?" Nope - active listening builds rapport, understanding, and trust with those you interact with on a regular basis. For instance: nodding along to what your boss or coworker says without really understanding their meaning can create miscommunication and errors- no one wants to be the one responsible! Furthermore, active listening shows respect for someone's thoughts and opinions- that's an invaluable win in both work and personal situations!

Now it's time to get down to business - what exactly does active listening entail? Well, I'm glad you asked.

- First and foremost: don't multitask while trying to listen actively - put away your phone, stop typing your email, and focus solely on the dialogue taking place in front of you.

- Body Language: Lean in slightly, make eye contact, and nod occasionally to demonstrate engagement and let others know you're here and willing to talk. These small gestures communicate a powerful message: I am here and ready for business."

- Do Not Interrupt: Though difficult, refraining from interrupting can be challenging if your ideas or counterarguments come pouring out at any moment. Wait for the speaker to finish before interjecting your thoughts or providing counterarguments.

- Reflect: From time to time, it may be useful to repeat back what you've heard - for instance by saying something like, "So, what you're saying is..." This reassures the speaker that they are being understood correctly while also giving both of you an opportunity to clarify any misconceptions if necessary.

- Ask Questions: Once it is your turn to speak, use questions as an opportunity for further understanding and engagement with the speaker's remarks. Doing this shows your engagement while also unearthing more nuanced points they might not have initially addressed.

- Don't Judge: For effective active listening, set aside all judgments at the door. Even if you disagree with what the person has to say, give them the benefit of doubt as you discuss topics together.

In conclusion, sum up what has been discussed, to demonstrate your attentive listening skills and ensure both parties leave with something tangible from this exchange.

Psychology and counseling use a term called "holding space," which refers to being physically, mentally and emotionally present for someone. Through active listening you're providing that space; not thinking about groceries or worrying how to fix that glitch in your project but being fully dedicated to understanding another human being at this moment - something with big ramifications! It can have tremendous effects.

Being honest: active listening can be challenging at times. It may require effort and patience in order to engage on this deep level as much as possible - your relationships and career will thank you.

Looking to enhance your listening game? Give these exercises a try:

• The 3-Minute Drill: Listen intently for three minutes as someone talks about anything--books read, movies seen, plans for the weekend--while actively not speaking yourself. Once they have spoken your job is to listen without speaking back then summarize their comments by repeating what has been said back out loud.

• Emotional Echo: Listen as someone shares an emotional experience and reflect back their words to capture not only their thoughts, but also their emotions.

• Regain Focus: Pay close attention during your next conversation to when your mind wanders from what was being discussed and note what distracted you - then redirect back your focus on it!

• Feedback Loop: Following each discussion, request feedback on your listening skills - were you engaged, did you interrupt or ask insightful questions? Use this information as a basis for future conversations.

Active listening doesn't just benefit yourself or those around you; its benefits extend far beyond this. When people feel heard and understood, they're more likely to extend this same kindness toward others - which fosters an environment of openness, mutual respect, and collaboration - something invaluable in any work setting. So not only are you improving your communication skills - you are contributing towards creating a healthier work environment with increased productivity; perhaps inspiring someone else along the way too!

So now that you understand all about active listening, it's time to put it into practice! Don't regret taking time out to hone this important skill; it will transform the quality of conversations, strengthen relationships, and bolster professional standing; all it requires is lending an ear-- actively.

6.3.2 Assertiveness vs. Aggressiveness

Do take a step back for a second: have you been in meetings or social settings where someone dominates all conversation and talks over people without regard for other viewpoints, creating an atmosphere of aggressiveness? On the flipside is someone who speaks confidently while making their point clearly while respecting other's viewpoints - that would be assertiveness! But it isn't always that simple so let's explore all aspects of assertive versus aggressive behaviors, especially within work settings.

Before we get into the details of assertiveness, let's define it first.

- Assertiveness: This term refers to being self-assured and confident without being aggressive. Psychologists consider assertiveness one of the healthiest communication styles: you express your needs, wants, feelings, and beliefs openly while respecting others' feelings and needs.

- Aggressiveness: Aggression is a method of expression used to further our own interests at the expense of others, often at their expense. Aggression often ends up winning out while everyone else loses.

Understanding these definitions is the cornerstone of successful communication. Knowing their difference affects how effectively you interact with colleagues, bosses, clients or even friends and family members.

Now, let's be fair: assertiveness and aggression aren't the only forms of communication out there; other modes exist, like passive or passive-aggressive approaches as well. Being passive involves going along with what other people want in order to avoid conflict while passive-aggressiveness is sneakier; you appear to agree but may later undermine what was agreed upon. Being aware of all these additional styles gives you a full palette of human interaction skills at your disposal, helping you navigate workplace communication more easily.

So how do these communication styles influence the office atmosphere? They have an immense effect. Assertiveness creates an environment in which ideas can be freely exchanged and everyone feels heard; aggressiveness on the other hand creates a toxic culture, driving down morale and productivity - no one likes feeling like their voice doesn't count!

Let's drill down into what makes assertiveness so golden. A few key principles to keep in mind:

- Clarity: Make your statements completely understood to maintain an assertive tone. Ambiguity can undermine an assertive approach.

- Empathy: Strive to understand where another is coming from without necessarily agreeing with their viewpoint; just acknowledge it and acknowledge their perspective.

- Balance: Seeking common ground should never just benefit one side - finding mutually beneficial middle grounds should also be the goal.

- Confidence: Speak with confidence if you want anyone else to believe what you say. Respect: Treat others with dignity even if their views differ from yours; always respect their rights and opinions even when there's disagreement between the parties involved.

Be careful, though. Sometimes what starts as assertiveness can tip into aggressiveness without you even realizing it. Signs this might be happening:

- Interrupting Others: You're so excited to make your point that you don't let others finish speaking.

- Disregarding Opinions: You start to think your viewpoint is the only one that matters.

- Physical Cues: Your body language becomes dominant, like standing over someone while they are seated.

- Tone: Your tone of voice becomes harsh or strident.

How can you navigate this tricky territory? Self-awareness and emotional intelligence can help. Practice can develop these essential abilities.

Let's turn our focus around and consider aggressiveness. Although the person may appear in control, their actions often stem from feelings of insecurity or fear - this shouldn't excuse their behavior, but understanding this aspect can help you address them more efficiently.

Do not be misled: aggression comes with a high cost. It can lead to workplace conflicts, damaged relationships and professional setbacks - in extreme cases it could cost your job! Recognizing and correcting aggressive tendencies from both yourself and others are essential steps towards maintaining workplace peace and productivity.

If you are dealing with aggressive behavior either from yourself or others, here are some strategies:

- Stay Calm: Aggressive individuals want you to feel intimidated and angry so don't give them that power! Instead, remain peaceful.

- Set Boundaries: Set clear boundaries regarding what behavior will be accepted from others; otherwise who will?

- Seek Mediation: Sometimes an outside perspective can provide essential clarity.

- Reflect and Adjust: After an aggressive encounter, take some time to analyze what went wrong and consider ways you could handle things more effectively in future interactions. Professional Guidance: In extreme circumstances, don't hesitate to seek professional assistance such as HR.

Remember this in the workplace: assertiveness is your friend. No matter whether it's during a meeting, presentation, or simply conversation at the water cooler - being assertive can only benefit you as it makes for better communications, more efficient team playback, and perhaps an overall happier working experience.

- Role-Play: Engage in roles where you practice stating your needs clearly and politely. I Statements: To remain assertive when assertiveness may not come easily for you, try framing them as personal responsibility instead of simply complaining that people don't listen; for instance "I feel unheard" instead of saying, "You aren't listening to me".

- Active Listening: Actively take in what others are telling you without formulating responses at the same time they are speaking.

- Non-Verbal Cues: Pay attention to your body language by standing tall, maintaining eye contact, and using open gestures.

- Feedback Loop: Seeking feedback from trusted people is the only way to accurately evaluate how well you're doing in life and business.

No doubt this was a lot of information to take in, but understanding the differences between assertiveness and aggression is critical for effective communication. So begin honing your assertiveness skills now, and experience first-hand how they alter interactions for the better!

So there you have it! Assertiveness is the cornerstone of effective communication while aggressiveness can quickly turn into toxic environments and strain relationships. Recognize and adjust for these differences so you can navigate interpersonal relationships like a pro.

Part 7: BONUS:

A New Version of You in 30 Days

7.1 The 30-Day Plan

Congratulations on making it this far in your learning! Great work! But let's be realistic; knowledge alone won't do anything to move things along. Enter The 30-Day Plan--a practical, down-to-earth strategy designed to jumpstart your journey towards a revamped you. No magical transformation here; simply put into action all that you've learned gradually over 30 days and gradually apply it with bite-size steps that work.

Are You Wondering Why 30 Days?" 30 days is an optimal length of time for building habits without losing momentum. Research suggests it takes 21 days on average for new behaviors to form; we provide 30 as an extra push and grace period for refining and optimizing them further. Take a peek at this overview:

Week One is dedicated to setting a foundation and taking baby steps forward, while Weeks 2-4 focus on building upon it while fine-tuning as you go.

Don't worry; we will explore these phases more deeply in later chapters, but for now keep this in mind: each week will feature unique focus areas and tasks designed to help bring about the change you desire.

What areas will we focus on? In accordance with what you already know, we will cover cognitive patterns, social interactions, workplace dynamics, and general well-being.

Our daily tasks, reflections, mini projects, and "me time" activities will serve as means for accomplishing this objective - not simply doing stuff; rather we are engaging in metacognition!

Measure what you can't track, so get set for some tracking action. Choose whatever format works for you: notebook, digital app or sticky notes on your bathroom mirror - whatever suits you best will help ensure a tangible record of your progress and act as a powerful source of motivation.

Life can be unpredictable, and rigid plans often fall apart under its strain. That's why this 30-day plan includes some wiggle room: missed an activity? No worries; just make up the task on another day. Want to switch up activities as long as they still meet the weekly focus.

This journey doesn't have to be undertaken alone; there's no need for you to go it alone. Share your plan with someone trustworthy--perhaps it be friends, family members or coworkers--to provide gentle nudges when needed or virtual high fives when completed successfully. This accountability partner could offer helpful support throughout.

7.1.1 Week 1: Setting the Foundation

Hello Trailblazer! Welcome to Week 1 of your 30-Day Plan. It is now time to roll up our sleeves, dig in our heels, and lay the groundwork for what promises to be an extraordinary journey ahead. No skyscraper may be constructed here, but something even greater may take shape: A stronger, more resilient you. So this week is about setting that foundation.

Before you think "Foundation? Who needs that already," take a moment and consider why this step is essential. When building a sandcastle, do you start by building intricate towers and delicate windows first? No. Instead, pack down wet sand to form a base. Without it, those towers would soon crumble away. Similarly, personal development journeys require creating a strong base upon which to build more complex habits or strategies later. Without such a solid base in place, such as personal development journeys could come crashing down on their faces before beginning their development journeys - without which could result in failure of both kinds.

Let's begin our personal development journey by cultivating self-awareness. Self-awareness is a fundamental tenet of personal development; it allows you to recognize where change needs to take place in the first place. Over the next couple of days, take some time for introspection - be it writing down thoughts, doodling them on paper, recording voice notes or simply contemplating during a long walk; whatever works for you - but just make sure that whatever method you choose includes introspection of self and examine strengths weaknesses, triggers and joys within. Remember this shouldn't be judged but rather observed for its own sake.

Building a foundation means creating a framework, or set of routines, you can count on. Maybe this has felt limiting before; here's the thing though - routines don't need to be rigid; they can act as flexible scaffolds that give your day structure. Instead of setting a rigid 6am wakeup time or having one fixed menu option available daily for example?

Simon Sinek advocates starting with your "Why." Your 'Why" should serve as more than a motivational catchphrase; it should serve as your true motivator, propelling forward every time. Reconnect with it whenever you feel stuck or demotivated and it will provide strength to keep moving forward.

Goal setting should follow suit and should be made achievable through setting goals that are SMART: Specific, Measurable, Achievable, Relevant and Time-bound. Finding a balance between challenging yourself and being realistic when setting attainable goals requires writing them down and keeping them visible; they represent not just aspirations but a roadmap!

Take this week as an opportunity to practice mindfulness! Mindfulness isn't some far-out Eastern concept - it's simply about being present and fully engaging in the moment - no need for lengthy sit-down meditation sessions; even 5-minute breathing exercises can set the scene for greater mindfulness throughout your day!

Relationships are indispensable. Make it a goal this week to connect with those that matter in your life by reaching out via text, call, or coffee date - these interactions provide your social safety net, so it is crucial to nurture them regularly with authentic interactions between each of the individuals. Nourishment requires being yourself rather than creating an artificial version of yourself which other people expect of you.

Balance can be an elusive concept. A common question: "how can I find a good balance between work, social life, health issues and hobbies and other responsibilities that need my attention?" There's no simple answer but one thing's certain: extreme swings either way won't last; so aim for moderation in all actions taken.

Remember, the plan is an evolving entity. Keep tabs on what's working and what isn't, adjusting as necessary if needed - this week should also teach you valuable skills for adapting as your plan develops further.

By the end of Week 1, you've laid not only foundational blocks but also laid the first layer of your personal development structure. By this stage, it's all about setting yourself up to succeed over the coming weeks; by giving yourself something solid to stand on. Don't worry; three more exciting and transformative weeks lie ahead - so feel proud about all you've accomplished and look forward to what lies ahead - don't take anything for granted - enjoy every second! And get excited; there is much more exciting stuff ahead - don't let anyone tell you otherwise - let alone watching it all happen before long!

7.1.2 Week 2-4: Building and Refining

Hello Future Star! Congratulations on making it through Week 1, where you laid the essential foundation. Now it is time to build and refine it, adding layers, features and details that turn it into a beautifully-crafted structure - like how a mosaic becomes increasingly vivid with each added piece, so too will your personal growth journey blossom during these weeks!

Let's continue our building metaphor: You now have a solid base on which to build upon; now comes the hard part - selecting materials, choosing colors and deciding on architectural elements that define who you are as an individual. All these decisions represent shaping and refining habits, strategies and skills in ways we might never imagine possible!

Week two is Habit Week--but these are no ordinary habits; these are keystone habits! These special practices can transform your life in multiple ways. Making your bed daily, for instance, has been linked with increased productivity and better mental health. Start by selecting keystone habits that best align with your goals and lifestyle; don't just pick popular ones without considering what resonates best for you personally.

Now, habits don't form overnight - be patient. Additionally, remember the goal is not simply to establish but maintain consistency over time using techniques such as habit stacking (adding new habits to existing ones) to keep momentum going and build lasting habits - it is better to have five consistent ones than 20 inconsistent ones!

Week 3--Skill Week--is about becoming more proficient at one specific skill that you believe will bring substantial improvement to your life, such as time management or emotional intelligence - even cooking healthy meals could benefit! Explore this area deeply. There are numerous resources out there from YouTube tutorials to online courses and books; utilize them actively as you practice this skill and apply it in real-life scenarios.

Week 4 is "Refinement Week," when you will refine and fine-tune. Picture yourself going around with a paintbrush to touch up any spots where the color has faded or chipped away. In Week 4, take stock of how well your habits and skills have developed since starting the challenge; assess what works and where adjustments need to be made; seek feedback from trusted family and friends and seek their input on areas for improvement that you hadn't considered before; this external perspective might provide insights you hadn't considered previously.

Stay mindful during these weeks. By now, you should have established some form of mindfulness practice - perhaps some deep breathing or short meditation sessions--but take it one step further by making mindfulness part of routine activities like eating or walking - it will bring immense clarity!

Keep a journal during these weeks; document everything-- your struggles, successes, insights and questions--that makes up your journey. Not only does keeping track help keep you on the right path but reflecting back can be extremely encouraging and motivating!

Hey, this journey doesn't need to be undertaken alone! Don't underestimate the power of social support; an "Accountability Buddy" can make an enormous difference. They serve as someone you check in with regularly in order to discuss progress, challenges, strategies etc. They don't necessarily need to be on a similar journey but must show genuine interest in helping your growth by offering constructive criticism.

Failure is inevitable in life, but let's change how we view failure: rather than seeing it as the end, see it as something to learn from and adapt accordingly. Failure should be seen not as the final word but as valuable data gathered along the way that should help steer your efforts in a better direction. So when something goes wrong don't fall into self-criticism mode immediately: rather take some time to assess why something went wrong before altering your approach accordingly.

Weeks 2-4 offer an overview of what lies ahead, but keep in mind this process is ongoing; even after these weeks have concluded, changes should still be maintained and tweaked here and there if needed. It's like caring for a garden; watering, trimming, and sometimes replanting seeds must all take place regularly in order to see real results.

At the conclusion of Week 4, reward yourself. Don't make it about binging on unhealthy stuff; rather do something meaningful that recognizes all your hard work - perhaps a small retreat, self-care day, or purchasing that book you've had your eye on for weeks could do just fine!

Your effort this week is more than simply passing time; you are slowly evolving into your best possible self. That alone is revolutionary! Keep building, refining, and developing as the best is yet to come!

7.2 Tracking Your Progress

But why track progress? At first blush, this may seem unnecessary; after all, positive change in my life should suffice as evidence of progress. But tracking is more than measuring outcomes: it's about recognizing patterns, bottlenecks and celebrating small wins that would otherwise go unnoticed. Pacing matters here - to maintain consistent progress requires real, actionable data which should help guide this effort. So how should we approach tracking?

Apps have become an indispensable resource in our hyper digitized age. From tracking calorie intake and time management to analytics and reminders, digital tools offer us convenience like never before. If journaling or marking on a calendar suits you better than apps do though, that might just work as well!

Keep your goals specific when setting them and monitoring progress, rather than setting vague ones like, "I want to improve my time management." Instead, set something more measurable like, "I will devote the first two hours of each workday exclusively to high-priority tasks without checking email or social media - that way your progress is trackable!"

Tracking doesn't just involve tallying up victories; it also involves understanding setbacks. Perhaps you have noticed that while weekday workouts tend to go well, weekends throw you off course more frequently; this pattern should give you the opportunity to delve further: What changed on weekends compared to weekdays? Was it social commitments or simply a more relaxed atmosphere that caused this deviation? Gaining insights into why setbacks occur is far more valuable than collecting unquestioned wins.

Establish a regular routine to review your progress - weekly, bi-weekly or even monthly is up to you - just make sure it happens consistently. When sitting down for this review session, bring all of yourself - no multitasking or distractions allowed! Just you, your records, and honest self-reflection. Be your own constructive critic as well as cheerleader; celebrate any small wins while not brushing aside setbacks under the carpet; instead bring them out into the light so they can be examined properly - much like cleaning out a closet!

Tracking isn't just a rearview mirror activity; it can also serve as an insightful lens into the future. Utilize these insights to adapt your strategies, make more intelligent decisions, and anticipate challenges you might encounter - something which makes tracking proactive rather than reactive, which can have hugely positive results for any organization.

Remember the Accountability Buddy? Your review ritual is an ideal opportunity to reunite with them and share your tracked data, hear their insights and collaborate on strategies - two minds often contribute more effectively towards growth than one alone!

Tracking your progress might not seem glamorous, but it is the cornerstone of personal development. Tracking will show just how far you've come and help steer you toward where you want to be going - keep at it; you are doing amazing!

7.2.1 Journaling Your Experience

Journaling can seem intimidating at first, especially to non-writers like myself who may feel they don't belong! Don't take my word for it though- journaling doesn't require becoming Shakespeare - far from it! Journaling simply provides an avenue to have conversations with yourself on paper or screen and can be life changing; offering you space to express who you really are without any apology while providing sanctuary for all your thoughts and emotions. Let's dive deeper into why journaling should become part of your tracker arsenal shall we?

Let's first address the obvious. Why is journaling when thinking things through is easy enough? Because thoughts can be fleeting; they come and go faster than you can say "self-improvement." Writing gives your thoughts tangible form that you can return to later for reflection or review; plus writing offers therapeutic benefits by giving you time and space to gather your thoughts and make sense of life's complexities.

What should you write about? There is no shortage of topics that could inspire writing: you could jot down goals for each day, week, or month; highlight or lowlight moments from your daily activities; track emotional states across time to gain insights into patterns in your emotional health; record epiphanies as they arise when traveling along your journey; these nuggets of wisdom could become invaluable resources in the future for you!

Let your journal reflect your evolving thoughts without being constrained by rigid structure; be as free-flowing and creative with it as you like. One day it could be a simple bullet list; on another it might include writing an emotional letter. Or you could experiment with sketching or doodling to capture certain feelings or concepts. Keep it unique; stay true to who you are!

One approach that may help is asking yourself questions such as, "What made me happy today?" and "What challenges me?" Doing this can act like having a guided dialogue with yourself; you might be amazed by what emerges. Using questions can help uncover hidden aspects of experiences and emotions buried deep within.

Don't feel pressured into writing epic sagas every evening; even just writing down a few lines can make an incredible difference. What matters most is creating a consistent routine. Journal daily, weekly, or at some other interval; making this part of your routine allows you to recognize trends and patterns over time - leading us to our second point!

Like reviewing other tracking data, set aside time to go over your journal entries. You'd be amazed what a simple trip down memory lane reveals - perhaps you'll identify themes or obstacles which need addressing proactively, while simply seeing your growth will serve as an incredible morale booster.

Make sure your journal remains secure and private. Treat it like your sanctuary, free from judgment from yourself or anyone else. Whether using digital software with password protection or keeping physical books safe in an undisclosed place, uphold its integrity to maintain this safe haven.

7.2.2 Using Apps for Monitoring

Alright, tech-savvy friends, this one's for you. Let's talk about the digital frontier of tracking your progress: apps. Now, I'm not saying you should ditch your handwritten journals or good ol' Excel sheets, but if you're someone whose phone is basically an extension of your hand, why not leverage that? Apps can be incredibly efficient in monitoring your progress, and their functionalities are almost as limitless as your ambitions. So, how can you navigate this expansive universe of self-improvement tools? Let's dive right in!

Prior to diving into the app store labyrinth, define exactly what you need help tracking. Is it mental well-being, physical fitness, time management or goal setting that needs addressing? Whatever it is, knowing exactly what your requirements are is key in selecting an appropriate tool.

Once you know exactly what features are important, it's time to pick and choose. From habit-tracking streaks to complex analytics, different apps offer various functions. Take your time exploring each option before making a final decision - many offer basic versions for free so that you can test drive their features before committing.

Simple is always best! Your app's user interface should make life simpler, not more challenging. Opt for one with an intuitive design that doesn't require you to hold a Ph.D. in Computer Science in order to operate.

Synchronizing data across devices can be a huge boon in today's connected world, enabling you to track progress easily whether on a phone, tablet, or computer. But if Big

Brother creepiness isn't your cup of tea, consider installing an app that provides local storage instead.

Do not forget to ask whether the app allows for export or backup of data, especially as you gain more insights into yourself through personal growth journey. Losing all that hard-won knowledge due to random glitches on a phone would be devastating!

Some may love them; others don't care for them, but most tracking apps come equipped with some sort of notification feature that you can customize to meet your individual needs - be it daily reminders for input of mood data or weekly progress updates; make sure it fits with what works for you!

Your personal development journey is highly intimate, so make sure that the app you choose takes its role of protecting your privacy seriously - read their privacy policy, look into their data handling processes and read user reviews to spot any red flags.

Last but certainly not least, make sure that the app integrates well with other tools or platforms you already use - for instance if you have a fitness tracker you may want an app that can pull data directly from it. The more seamlessly your new app fits into your existing ecosystem, the smoother will be its experience for you.

There you go! With goal-setting apps and mood trackers aplenty, the app universe brims with resources aimed at helping you become your ideal self. Navigating this digital realm may be daunting at first, but with some careful searching you're bound to uncover an invaluable app to aid your journey towards self-improvement. Happy tracking!

7.3 Celebrating Your Achievements

Nothing compares to that incredible feeling when you accomplish something meaningful - whether that means sticking with a new habit for seven days straight, making an important choice that paid off, or finally finding work-life harmony. So give yourself credit; however, let's go beyond simple self-congratulatory celebration and explore ways we can recognize our achievements - these milestones serve as epilogues in your personal growth story which continues onward.

Wait a second - why make such a fuss? Celebrating your accomplishments doesn't just bring happiness; it also helps improve psychological well-being by offering closure for all of the hard work and effort put into achieving goals. Like adding the cherry to top off a delicious treat; celebrating is like adding that memorable flourish to make it all worthwhile!

Let's briefly delve into neurotransmitters. Achievements typically result in the release of dopamine, the "feel-good" hormone. Dopamine helps motivate us and increase pleasure; by celebrating your accomplishments you amplify its release, telling your brain "hey that felt awesome - let's do it again!" And not only are you improving your mood - you are setting the foundation for future successes as well!

Assuming you didn't strike an incredible multimillion-dollar deal or pen the next bestseller isn't necessary - even minor accomplishments can have a lasting effect on both your well-being and confidence. Even managing to exercise three times this week despite your busy schedule deserves recognition, while finally taking care of a pile of paperwork on your desk is worth celebrating - every small win counts towards moving in the right direction, so acknowledging them helps maintain momentum.

Celebration doesn't need to be extravagant or grandiose - all it requires is taking a moment and reveling in your success! Spoil yourself with something you enjoy such as delicious dessert, new book or TV series episode... Or how about hosting a dance-off in your living room without judgment from others!

If you prefer something more social, share your accomplishment with family or friends and revel in their positive reinforcement to reinforce your sense of achievement and joy; surely shared happiness makes life richer?

Make celebrating an intentional act. Set aside some time each week or month to think back over what you've achieved and the lessons learned along the way - an introspective exercise can offer invaluable insights that fuel future endeavors. Jot down or verbalize your reflections - hearing yourself list off all of your achievements is highly empowering.

Take note, though: while celebrating your achievements is great, keep it sustainable. Splurging on an extravagant vacation every time you complete something might set yourself up for future financial distress (unless of course, you happen to be an unwitting millionaire!).

Remember the goal is to enhance your well-being and set yourself up for future successes. Flashy celebrations may offer immediate gratification but consider their long-term consequences before choosing meaningful yet sustainable methods of commemorating achievements.

7.3.1 Recognizing Milestones

Milestones mark your journey, providing anchors in your sea of personal development. By tracking your progress and noting special moments that represent achievements substantial enough, milestones provide meaning on which your path can rely. So let's unwrap this idea of milestones to understand why they're more than just mental high-fives!

First things first: What constitutes a milestone? Simply put, it is an event or achievement which marks a turning point in your journey and marks its conclusion and transition into another phase - whether that means getting that promotion you've been eyeing, or reaching an emotional intelligence level whereby you are capable of adeptly managing conflicts.

But why should we bother recognizing milestones? It can be easy to get caught up in the endgame, focusing solely on reaching our final destination, but individual milestones serve as milestones along your journey, providing mini-validations of progress along your journey and providing confirmation that we're moving in the right direction - like having your personal GPS give a thumbs-up when we reach a major goal.

Milestones come in many forms and scales. There are performance milestones--such as finishing an important project at work--that deserve recognition, while there are also emotional ones like conquering longstanding fears or phobias, or 'anti-milestones' where not doing something becomes an achievement; something as small as not procrastinating for one week counts! All need recognition!

When commemorating a milestone, take time to analyze its components. Was success achieved through skill, luck or timing - or some combination thereof? Understanding its components allows you to replicate it again later - setting in motion an ongoing cycle of success!

Celebration milestones have an outward effect, too. By noting your small victories and celebrating them with others, you are setting an example and reminding everyone around you of how every step counts - whether in work, relationships or personal development. Your actions could encourage others to start recognising their milestones too!

Remarking milestones should be undertaken thoughtfully. Consider making it into a small ritual: light a candle, make your favorite cup of coffee, play some upbeat tunes and reflect upon what milestones have been reached in a meaningful manner - even if they seem minor on paper! Get into the zone to fully recognize their magnitude despite appearances to the contrary.

7.3.2 Rewarding Yourself Appropriately

Now comes the fun part! After all of the hard work and possibly even some bloodshed (we won't ask), it's finally time for rewards! But hold off: before booking yourself an extravagant two-week holiday to Bali as an incentive, let's talk about rewarding yourself appropriately. Rewards should enhance our sense of achievement while propelling us toward our next great venture with gusto; therefore let's delve into this art of rewarding oneself properly.

As no two milestones are alike, neither should their rewards. A fitting reward should reflect the significance of each milestone: for instance if you ace an important presentation at work, maybe a weekend getaway would do; while keeping to your diet could merit something like an evening out with friends as a celebratory token. Making sure your reward fits within context ensures you're not over or understating your achievements.

There's a novel idea here: rewards that not only make you feel good but also advance your journey. Imagine reaching a milestone in your physical fitness journey and treating yourself to an extravagant meal; but why not invest instead in a high-end blender for smoothies or dumbbells for home gym use instead? Such rewards serve two functions simultaneously--pleasure and progress!

Now let's do some serious thinking. Did you know that dopamine released from an appropriately timed, well-chosen reward can actually make future milestones easier to reach? When we reward ourselves appropriately, it doesn't just signify patting ourselves on the back; rather it reinforces a behavioral loop which makes taking on subsequent challenges easier - all this while seeming like mere indulgence, yet investing in future success! Pretty cool stuff?

Now, this doesn't mean lavishing yourself with rewards every time something good happens; timing is essential. Some experts advocate a 'variable reward schedule,' where rewards vary in timing and type, to keep things interesting; others suggest using more linear approaches that follow a predictable timeline; experiment and see what works for you best; either way, make sure not to let rewards overshadow milestones themselves!

Say you give yourself a treat after completing one month of clean eating - which is perfectly appropriate - be mindful that it doesn't become an excuse for slipshod practices; an appropriately chosen reward should enhance rather than undermine all your hard work. A reward should serve to celebrate rather than undermine milestones you've reached.

Reward yourself appropriately; by showing that you value yourself and your achievements. Doing this sets an important precedent for approaching challenges and milestones in the future with grace and optimism - your relationship with yourself will thank you.

Conclusion

As we reach the end of this amazing journey together, I want you to give yourself some much-deserved credit: making it this far shows commitment and the potential for real change - an achievement not everyone can claim to achieve - so please accept my sincerest congratulations for making it this far.

Starting out by unraveling who and what you want, we began this journey by uncovering who and what emotions play a role in. After that came mastering emotions - essential components in life-quality! Next came managing work-life balance, stress management, communication skills enhancement and adaptability/change management/growth mindset development/flexing your growth mindset muscles! All these chapters/paragraphs poured in are not simply chapters; each section provided vital life skills which have enabled you to become an overall more well-rounded, resilient individual - congratulations!

Before we part ways, let's be clear: Personal development is a long game. It can be tempting to get caught up in the excitement of new beginnings; setting goals can feel invigorating at first. Yet as time wears on, this initial burst of energy may begin to dissipate - perhaps you have already experienced this phenomenon as you worked through exercises and strategies from this book - yet consistent, focused effort remains crucial for long-term success.

Motivation can be fleeting; it comes and goes. But discipline remains reliable even after everyone else has left the party. Remember how we discussed creating structures and routines? They serve as scaffolding for discipline. So when your motivation dwindles, discipline will help carry you forward.

As you step forth with new knowledge and skills, keep learning a lifelong pursuit. There will always be something new around the corner to consider; keep up that sense of curiosity we discussed while developing a growth mindset. Make it a point to revisit the exercises in this book periodically; perhaps set an alarm so as to do it on time each time through. With each read through you may discover nuggets of insight you missed the first time around!

Personal development shouldn't just benefit yourself. It should benefit everyone you come into contact with as well -

your partner, friends, coworkers, family and loved ones all gain from it as you become a better version of yourself. Think of personal growth as the ripple effect - as yours progresses, reach out your hand and help lift others up as well.

Feel free to adapt any concepts or strategies presented in this book so they best suit your circumstances; making your path truly personalized is not only acceptable--it is encouraged!

At times of stress or uncertainty, the temptation to fall back into old patterns may be strong. When that occurs, revisit your "Why". Your "Why" should be at the core of all decisions to seek change; allow it to guide you through any confusion and bring you back on course.

Now, a word about courage. Admitting one's shortcomings requires tremendous bravery; even more so when taken further. By embarking on this path to self-improvement, you have shown incredible fortitude - let that sink in for a moment and appreciate what an impressive feat it truly was!

Time has come for you to close this chapter--both physically and figuratively. Your next stage of journey has begun now, and I couldn't be more proud. While the book may end here, its journey doesn't.

Thank you for inviting me into your incredible journey toward personal development. Now that you have all of the tools and strategies in your arsenal, go forth and make life an extraordinary adventure - the world awaits its pearls!

Your journey awaits! Just know that when significant milestones or "aha!" moments arise, think back on our time together in these pages - I will be cheering for you each step of the way!

PIP

- Enqu: 0800 587 0932 + changes.
- capita .:
- Make the call : 0800 232 1271 (help)
  photocopies not originals.
  NI Number on each page on additional evidence
  full name.